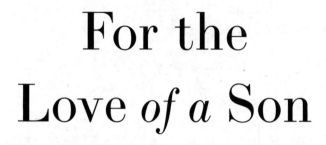

For the
Love *of a* Son

A Memoir of Addiction, Loss, and Hope

SCOTT OAKE

WITH MICHAEL HINGSTON

Published by Simon & Schuster

New York   Amsterdam/Antwerp   London   Toronto   Sydney   New Delhi

SIMON &
SCHUSTER
CANADA

A Division of Simon & Schuster, LLC
166 King Street East, Suite 300
Toronto, Ontario M5A 1J3

In order to protect privacy, some names in this book have been changed.

All photos courtesy of the author except pages 193, 195, 212, 215, 218,
and 235, which are courtesy of the Bruce Oake Recovery Centre, and
page 225, which is courtesy of the Government of Manitoba.

This Simon & Schuster Canada edition January 2025

SIMON & SCHUSTER CANADA and colophon are
registered trademarks of Simon & Schuster, LLC

For information about special discounts for bulk purchases,
please contact Simon & Schuster Special Sales
at 1-800-268-3216 or CustomerService@simonandschuster.ca.

Interior design by Ruth Lee-Mui

Manufactured in the United States of America

1   3   5   7   9   10   8   6   4   2

Library and Archives Canada Cataloguing in Publication
Title: For the love of a son : a memoir of addiction, loss, and hope / Scott Oake.
Names: Oake, Scott, author.
Description: Simon & Schuster Canada edition.
Identifiers: Canadiana (print) 20240352297 | Canadiana (ebook) 20240352300 |
ISBN 9781668045473 (softcover) | ISBN 9781668045480 (EPUB)
Subjects: LCSH: Oake, Bruce, 1985–2011—Drug use. | LCSH: Oake, Scott—Family.
| LCSH: Drug addicts—Family relationships—Canada—Biography. | LCSH: Sons—
Drug use—Canada—Biography. | LCSH: Fathers and sons—Canada—Biography.
| LCSH: Parents of drug addicts—Canada—Biography. | LCSH: Sons—Death—
Psychological aspects. | LCGFT: Biographies. | LCGFT: Autobiographies.
Classification: LCC HV5805.O25 O25 2025 | DDC 362.29092/2—dc23

ISBN 978-1-6680-4547-3
ISBN 978-1-6680-4548-0 (ebook)

For Bruce and Anne and for every addict who's ever had the courage to fight the horrid disease that is addiction.
—Scott Oake

If you or someone you know is struggling with addiction,

I encourage you to contact us. Go to Bruceoakerecovery.ca.

Do it right now, if you need to.

Someone will answer you, I promise.

—Scott Oake

Contents

Prologue

This Place

On a warm summer evening in June 2023, I walk into a bright, modern facility in the West End of Winnipeg to attend an alumni-milestone event at the Bruce Oake Recovery Centre—what the staff and participants informally call Birthday Night.

Bruce Oake is an addiction treatment centre that's named after my oldest son. Bruce died of a drug overdose more than a decade earlier, but he's never far from my mind—especially here. As I walk through the centre's front doors, I see the glass memorial case that holds Bruce's remains, and I rub the top of it to say hello, the same way I do every time I enter or leave the building.

From there I make my way to the gymnasium, navigating through a crowd that's getting larger by the minute. Along the way I mingle with the guys, and shake as many hands as I can. I also make a point of calling people by their names, because it means a lot to guys who've been on the fringes of society for so long to have someone remember who they are. Luckily, my memory is pretty good on this front. For the life of me I cannot tell you the final score in a hockey game two minutes after going off the air, but I can easily recall the names of dozens of guys who've been through the program at Bruce Oake. When I finally get to the gym's entrance, I see rows of folding chairs facing the stage, where a podium and microphone are set up. It's almost showtime, so I quietly take a seat off to the side and wait for the ceremony to begin.

When it comes to addiction and recovery, I'm not a professional. Far from it. Technically, I'm not even an employee at Bruce Oake. But as its cofounder, I am its biggest fan and supporter. That's why I find myself coming by the centre most days, eating lunch with the participants and working out in its gym. When Bruce first started using, as a teenager, Anne and I didn't have the slightest clue about addiction, and what a vicious disease it is. Nor did we understand that it was also a national crisis, with thousands of Canadians dying of overdose every year. After Bruce's death, Anne and I started asking how one might go about building a recovery centre, and we were told, "Build the kind of place a person would want to live." So that's exactly what we did. As a result, this centre is 43,000 square feet of warm and inviting space, bathed in natural light, with dozens of floor-to-ceiling windows overlooking a beautiful creek and trail system. It's the perfect place to reflect and heal.

There's an excited energy in the gym. In the world of recovery, your "birthday" is the date you stopped using, and we're all here tonight to celebrate three guys from the program who have achieved

a full year of sobriety—the first sixteen weeks as a resident of the recovery centre, completing the Bruce Oake program, and the rest of it
out in the world, taking the skills they learned in here and using them
to build a healthy new life for themselves. It's not an easy thing to
do, and tonight's ceremony is a recognition of that accomplishment.
Hanging in the rafters above us are dozens of customized Winnipeg
Jets jerseys, each one adorned on the back with the last name of a
graduate who's achieved a year sober, along with the same number
underneath: 1. Tonight we'll be lifting three more jerseys to the rafters, bringing the total number to more than fifty—pretty impressive,
considering the centre has barely been open two years.

The ceremony itself is just as celebratory. One graduate, who
seems a little nervous, reads his speech to the audience off his phone.
It consists of a series of bullet points, the first of which is, simply: "I
love this place." Another makes a joke about how he dreams of one
day taking his jersey to an actual Jets game, along with the other guys
from his recovery group. "Everyone there will be confused, because
nobody on the Jets wears number 1," he says. "But we'll know what
it means."

No matter their talents at public speaking, I find all of these men
and their speeches incredibly moving. They've been through something very difficult, and they've survived it. Now they're onstage ex-
pressing gratitude and sharing their stories in front of their friends,
family, and fellow alumni. But it's the third speaker tonight who really makes me choke up, because he reminds me so much of Bruce.
Like my son, this graduate comes from a well-off family, and enjoyed
the kind of privilege growing up that some people think protects
them from the dangers of addiction. Unfortunately, they're wrong.

Addiction knows no boundaries, not even socioeconomic ones, and it can come for anyone.

At moments like this, I can see Bruce in my mind so clearly: a strapping, 6'2", good-looking boy who got the best of Anne and me. He had dark brown hair, hazel eyes, and a thousand-watt smile that turned heads whenever he walked into a room. But it's funny. I sometimes find myself trying *not* to think of him, because if I do, it's easy to break down completely. I watch these graduates up there, beaming with pride, and can't help but think about how Anne and I had always dreamed that would one day be Bruce. At the same time, if he hadn't died, this place wouldn't exist. I'm so proud of everyone who has found success here, while also feeling the intense sadness that my son can never join them on that stage. There is a whole range of complicated emotions that can take over if I let them. Instead, I focus on the guys. That way, I don't become a puddle.

After the graduates have finished speaking, Terrence Morin, who was once a participant himself and is now a full-time employee of the centre, goes up to the mic. In some ways, Terrence is the polar opposite of Bruce—a heavily tattooed former gang member who for years was caught up in a life of violent crime. He still looks tough, but anyone who knows Terrence these days will tell you he's the nicest and most loyal guy in the world.

"Recovery is real," he tells the audience. "Brotherhood is real."

Next up is Greg Kyllo, the executive director of Bruce Oake, who speaks passionately about both the work the centre is doing and the work that is still ahead. "Word is spreading from coast to coast to coast about this world-class facility we have here in Winnipeg," he says, over a round of applause.

It's true—Bruce Oake receives phone calls from all across Canada, asking to join its waitlist. Demand is so high that, if a second centre were to magically open next door, its fifty beds would be full that same day.

When the speeches are done, a group of Bruce Oake alumni join the new graduates onstage, roughly two dozen guys from all kinds of backgrounds who may not have much in common besides their shared battle against addiction. But they're all standing up there together, hugging and laughing, brothers in recovery. It fills me with pride to see these men returning to their families, their friends, and society as a whole, optimistic about their futures and wanting to make a difference. I think to myself, *It's amazing how far they've come.*

It's a beautiful evening, and I wish Bruce were here to see it. I wish Anne were here, too.

This book is the story of a building, and a story of hope, both for those who helped make it a reality and for those who've walked through its front doors in search of a better life. It's also the story of grieving parents who wanted to do something to honour the memory of their son. But you can't really tell either of those stories without also telling the story of that son and what he went through. In order to really understand the Bruce Oake Recovery Centre, you first have to understand Bruce himself.

One

Love You Forever

I awoke on the morning of August 21, 1985, in a hotel room in Saint John, New Brunswick. It was an ungodly hour, and my phone was ringing. I blinked. It was barely daybreak in New Brunswick, which meant it was two hours earlier than in Manitoba. Right away I knew something was up. I stumbled out of bed and picked up the receiver.

It was my wife, Anne. "I think my water broke," she said.

My heart instantly jumped into my throat. "Are you sure?"

"Yes," she deadpanned. "Pretty sure."

Once the initial shock wore off, I realized that on some level I'd been expecting this call all along. I'm a sports broadcaster by profession, and for the last two weeks I'd been in town as one of the commentators covering the Canada Summer Games for the CBC. When I said yes to this particular trip, Anne was nine months pregnant with our first child, and I had a feeling I might need to return to Winnipeg sooner rather than later.

I usually spent weekdays in Winnipeg where Anne and I lived, and where I covered local sports for the evening news. On the weekends, I was often flown somewhere else in the country for an anthology show CBC used to make called *Sports Weekend*. But in between those two gigs, I would also get called upon to cover other major sporting competitions as they came along, including the Canada Summer Games, which was a good, high-profile assignment. I liked saying yes to these kinds of jobs. I was still at that hungry stage in my career where I wanted to go everywhere and do everything.

As the Games neared the end, we had both hoped she could hang on until I returned home. By the sounds of it, that wasn't going to happen.

"Where are you now?" I asked Anne.

"Well, I'm in the closet of the house on Essex." In other words, her parents' home.

I was still so groggy I wasn't sure I'd heard her right. "The closet? What are you doing in a closet?"

"I didn't want to upset anybody!" she said.

This was classic Anne, who was always thinking about others before herself. It was one of the things I loved about her. While I was away, she was staying with her parents and her uncle Jim, who was very important to her. Jim was the oldest of her mother's siblings, who had been caught in the polio epidemic of the 1950s. He ended up nearly a quadriplegic, with just enough mobility in one arm to operate his wheelchair. But Jim was also such a compassionate and intelligent person. His family used to joke that he was Google before there was Google.

And yet, despite being surrounded by her closest family members—even as her contractions were starting—Anne still took care not to bother them until it was absolutely necessary.

On the phone, I managed to convince her that the time was indeed now, and so she woke her mother up and they headed off together to the hospital. After I hung up, it really sunk in: I was about to become a father. This was no time to be sitting alone in a hotel room. I was half a country away and had to get back to Anne as quickly as possible.

These days, of course, the expectations are so different for fathers: you're probably going to be there not just throughout the labour process but also for at least a week or two afterwards. Back then, however, it was considered normal that I only managed to just get myself to St. Boniface Hospital in time.

I called up the CBC's business manager who was assigned to our show, and they arranged to put me on the next flight. I raced over to the airport, picked up the paper ticket that was waiting for me, and headed off to Winnipeg. There were no direct flights, however, so first I had to go to Montreal. As I went through the agonizingly slow process of boarding and deboarding, my mind was racing.

Anne and I had first met in the spring of 1977 on a blind date, of all things. At the time, François Riopel, my counterpart on the French side of CBC Manitoba, was going out with a girl who knew Anne, and we decided to go on a double date at Town N' Country, a former restaurant/nightclub in Winnipeg where Portage Place mall is now. They used to bring in bands in like Tommy James and the

Shondells, and Barbra Streisand played some of her first shows there as a teenager back in the '60s. I was a bit nervous about the date, but Anne and I hit it off right away. She was not only beautiful but also a pistol, the kind of person who could take the piss out of you in about ten seconds if she wanted to. It was a perfect match. We started dating right away, and three years later got married at Norwood United Church.

Anne and I had been married for four years and we'd been talking about having kids for half that time. I came from a big family, and I'd always liked the idea of having one of my own someday. But it had been difficult for Anne to get pregnant. We'd gone through the whole rigmarole of taking the temperature and monitoring the calendar for the best fertility windows. More than once, I'd received a frenzied phone call at noon: "Get home, I'm ovulating!"

In a futile attempt to steady my nerves, I downed a bunch of caffeine on the plane and was racing towards the exit doors the second the fasten-seatbelt signal was turned off. When I finally got to the hospital and found Anne's room, she'd already been in labour for nearly fifteen hours. She looked exhausted. I ran over and excitedly put my arms around her, and when Anne caught one whiff of my coffee breath, she said those beautiful words that every father-to-be dreams of hearing: "Get your fucking hands off me!"

A beautiful moment, I think you'll agree. But Anne was right. This was no time for a passionate embrace. The baby was coming.

As the labour went on, however, it was clear that Bruce wasn't moving that much. Plus, Anne was in a lot of pain. The doctors finally gave her an epidural, which helped, but as we approached midnight, the physician who was in charge of delivering the baby decided that we'd waited long enough. He announced he was going to use forceps to help get the baby out, and from there it wasn't long until Baby Bruce emerged—with a slightly oblong head, it must be said, but that quickly rounded back into shape. He also came out with a shock of dark hair, spiked out in all directions like an infant Johnny Rotten. Anne was sent off to the recovery room, while I sat up in the quiet night, cuddling our brand-new baby.

A lot of that day is a blur to me now, but I'll never forget the hour or so that Bruce and I sat there together. I remember racking my brain for nursery rhymes to sing to him as he slept, and ended up humming a bunch of nonsense while mentally hoping he wouldn't be able to tell the difference. The whole time, I looked at his tiny infant body, thinking, *This is it. Every decision we make for the rest of our lives will be with him in mind.* It was equal parts exhilaration and concern. My old life was over, and my new life as a parent was just beginning.

Then I went to the airport and got on a red-eye back to New Brunswick, where I finished calling the Canada Summer Games. What an idiotic decision on my part. What I *should* have done was tell my bosses that I wasn't coming back. I don't think they would have even questioned the decision. But that's just how things were back then. I was at a good place in my career, doing a lot of network assignments, and it felt like I had no choice but to keep going. (There may also have been a bit of ego involved. *How,* I thought, *would the Games survive without the great Scott Oake present?*)

Unfortunately, this type of thinking is all too common in my line of work. There's still a belief among a lot of people in media that you never pass on an assignment, because if you do, someone else will come along and do it better than you would've, and then you'll never get another opportunity again. You see this in the NHL, too, where players feel pressure to tough it out and keep playing through difficult situations because there are ten other guys on the roster waiting to take their job. Or so they think, anyway. Back then it was a very real concern, and it led me away from my son just a few hours after he was born.

We named our son Mckenzie Bruce Oake, after Anne's mother's maiden name and my beloved older brother.

I grew up in the working-class town of Sydney, Nova Scotia, as the second oldest of five kids in the 1950s. My younger siblings were Judy, Brad, and Stuart. My older brother, Bruce, was born with a condition called spina bifida, which is basically an opening in the back of the spinal column. If someone is born with spina bifida today, they're rushed straight into an operating room and that opening is closed up right away. Suffice to say it wasn't treated that way in the '50s. The opening in his spine was left untreated for a couple of months, until my aunt finally found a doctor way on the other side of Cape Breton Island, in Inverness County.

The doctor looked at Bruce's back and said, "Well, I don't know much about this, but I can see you're desperate, so I'll read up on it and come in tomorrow morning to do the operation." And that's what he did. Bruce remained a paraplegic, but if not for that operation, he would surely have died within months, or even weeks.

More than anything, Bruce was just a good person. As a kid I always followed him around and did whatever he did, because whatever he did usually turned out to be the right thing. As a university student, Bruce and a group of his friends somehow managed to get a government grant of nearly half a million dollars to run a program that provided recreation for people with mental disabilities. He was just driven to help, and I always admired that about him.

The pressure to work hard was instilled in all of us from a young age. My parents came from a generation where very few people ever went to university, and all they wanted was for their kids to do better than they had done. Sydney was a company town, and my dad, like all of the other dads, worked at the steel plant while my mom stayed home and raised all five of us kids. Walt, as I always called him, had a strong work ethic, which I like to think I've inherited. And my mom may have worked even harder than he did. She was a fairly even-keeled person, and she handled all of the household work in front of her with aplomb.

Walt had a pretty good job, but our family didn't have a lot of money. Bruce's condition required a lot of expensive, specialized medical care, and every year he and my dad flew to Montreal for operations at the Shriners Hospital. (Luckily for us, the organization covered their airfare.) We lived on a street in Sydney called Moxham Drive, in a co-op of eight identical houses, most of which were occupied by members of my extended family. It was a tight-knit little community, which was both good and bad. On the one hand, the street was always full of other kids to play with. On the other, everyone always knew everyone else's business.

When I got a bit older, Dad took a new job at a different steel company, and so our family moved to St. John's, Newfoundland, where Bruce and I both went on to attend Memorial University together. Because he'd had to spend so much time in hospital, Bruce fell a year behind in school, and so the two of us ended up in the same grade despite my being a year younger. That suited me just fine. And so when Bruce started hanging around the campus radio station, naturally I did, too. Eventually I got a shot filling in on a couple of sports and news hits, and from there I caught the broadcasting bug—or, as I like to say, I fell in love with the sound of my own voice.

Not long after that, I heard about a summer-relief job at the local CBC station. I was excited and sent over an application, but didn't hear anything back. A couple of weeks later, I figured it wouldn't hurt to call the station directly to follow up. The guy who answered the phone said, "Oh, right. Yours is actually the only application we got. So I guess you can start on Monday." If this story sounds a little far-fetched, keep in mind that broadcasting back then wasn't the distinguished career it is today. It was still seen as a kind of novelty—in fact, TV in Newfoundland was still black and white well into the '70s.

I ended up doing that summer-relief job for two summers, alongside my studies at Memorial. Then the station told me that one of their two full-time sportscasters had quit to go to law school. Don't ask me how I ended up getting the job, because my style at the time was to speak faster than the speed of light. I already thought I knew everything, and, if I had to, that I could get it all out in the world's longest sentence. For some reason they hired me anyway.

I'd always been interested in sports. From a young age I'd fancied myself an athlete, though in reality I was a poor one. And I had long been a voracious reader of anything related to hockey. As a teenager, I used to camp out by the front door every morning for our copy of the *Cape Breton Post* to be delivered, just so I could see whether Normie Ferguson had scored the night before. Ferguson was also from Sydney, and scored 34 goals in his rookie season for the Oakland Seals—he ended up losing the Calder race, but it was to Danny Grant, a fellow Maritimer, so I couldn't be *that* upset.

I was two years into my degree when I got the full-time job offer, and I knew my father wasn't going to be happy when he learned I was dropping out. I tried to placate him by promising I'd only do the broadcasting job for a couple of years, and then go back to finish my education. I'm not sure if he believed me. And I did actually take a couple of night courses when I first started working. But then, two years after leaving school, I was briefly recruited to work at CBC in Toronto, and from there moved to Winnipeg to replace the late great Don Wittman on the local sports beat. A few months after that, I was sent to the Olympics in Montreal.

After that, there was really no looking back.

Whenever I've told this story in public, I say that my dad continued to ask me every month until he died when I was going to finally go back to finish my degree, just so I had something to fall back on when CBC and *Hockey Night in Canada* finally figured out I was no good. In reality, it didn't happen quite that often—but he did keep bringing it up. I had to gently tell him, "It's a little late for that, Walt." And it was.

When I landed in Montreal to cover the Summer Olympics, I felt like my career was really taking off. Those Olympics happened to mark the first real leap for the CBC into what we call marathon broadcasting. Back in Munich in 1972, the network was still doing things like filling the primetime hours with prepackaged events that had already taken place. For the first-ever Canadian Olympics, however, it was a point of pride for them to be live on the air all day long: morning show, afternoon show, and evening show, with different commentators at every single venue.

At the time, I took my assignment as proof that I was on my way towards stardom, but looking back on it, I have to laugh. How many summer Olympic sports were there? Twenty? It's painfully obvious to me now that the CBC simply needed all hands on deck to cover such an ambitious broadcasting schedule. It's true that I was the youngest guy on the broadcast team, at just twenty-two years old, but my imminent rise to celebrity was perhaps a bit overinflated in my own mind. I got the call because everyone did.

Regardless, that confidence powered me through those Olympics broadcasts, and in particular one of my greatest achievements on the air.

I was assigned to cover wrestling alongside Ole Sorensen, who had actually competed in Munich and used to go running around the top of Mount Royal while I was still lying in bed. But that didn't faze me. I acted like such an expert during the broadcast that I managed to keep the actual wrestler quiet while doing almost all of the talking myself. In the heat of the moment, I considered it a great victory that I didn't need his help. (As one of my bosses at the CBC once told me, "Kid, the key to broadcasting is to be able to speak for an entire minute on a topic you know nothing about, and never repeat yourself.") Now, I'm mostly just surprised Ole didn't punch me in the face.

At the same time, that kind of ambition somewhat comes with the territory. My goal from early on was to do as many sports as I could and one day become a national network commentator. Most of the folks who get into this business are the same way. You start out trying to find work doing, say, play-by-play for junior B hockey. Then you graduate to junior A. Then, if you're really lucky, you make it to the pro level. But there aren't many network sports-commentator jobs to go around—and there were even fewer of them then. I was hoping I would one day rise to top, and I was willing to sacrifice to get there.

Of course, it's easier to make those sacrifices as a single man. Not so much as a husband and new father.

But God bless Anne, she never really complained. Not even when I left her and Bruce that first night in the hospital. There may have been a few wisecracks here and there over the years, but she never once laid down the law and asked me to make a choice. No matter whether I was off covering darts, or speed skating, or track and field, or trampoline, she always put my career first. And in the long term, it only worked out because of Anne's love for me, and her understanding that my career was important to me—and, by extension, to us as a family.

It was incredibly difficult for me to leave so soon after Bruce was born. But that sadness was matched, and then some, by the happiness I felt when I finally arrived back at home from the Canada Summer Games and saw Anne and Bruce waiting for me at the garage door of our family home. Suddenly, I wasn't just coming home to my wife anymore. Now it was Anne, standing there in this beautiful red flower dress, holding our son in her arms. We were a family. In that moment, I felt like I really had it all.

I treasured my time with Bruce just as much, especially because I

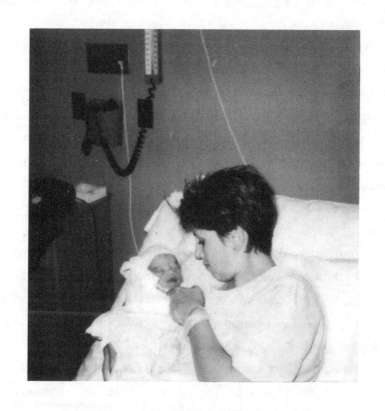

would spend the rest of my week yo-yoing between Winnipeg and the rest of the country. The way it worked back then is we would record *Sports Weekend* somewhere on-site, but then we'd have to go back to Toronto, where the show was edited and packaged, to produce the final mix. So those times at home, where it was just the three of us, were special.

Bruce really was a dream baby. He never fussed. He was even good in restaurants. And he certainly never had the kind of uncontrollable fits where you'd have to leave the room with him. Bruce's favourite book was Robert Munsch's *Love You Forever*, and Anne used to read it to him every night before bed. When she was done, she would close the book and say to him, "Love you, like you, see you in the morning."

Anne and I thought we'd hit the mother lode—and in many ways we did.

People had told us that once the baby was born our lives would never be the same. And they were right. Having a child fulfilled something inside me. I realized I'd always been drawn to the idea of fatherhood: I liked being around kids, and I'd even worked with the Winnipeg chapter of Big Brothers for a while. And of course I came from a family of five kids myself, which meant the household was always busy when I was growing up in the Maritimes. But having a child of my own was a whole new level of emotion and responsibility. I remember in those early days watching Bruce cuddling his baby blanket and marvelling at his potential. I used to think, *He could be anything. He could take the world by storm.*

Two

Patterns

Bruce was such a good baby in those early months. He slept so soundly that Anne used to wake up at 3 a.m. and put her finger under his nose, just to make sure he was breathing. You hear these stories about newborns who are so fussy, and require so much care, especially through the night, that their parents become zombies who aren't able to have any kind of life outside of childcare. It wasn't like that with us at all. Bruce was just calm and content, sleeping soundlessly for twelve hours every evening.

The one part I can take a bit of credit for is building the cradle that he slept in. I'd gotten the blueprint from the father of one of Anne's good friends, and her uncle Jim and I brought it up to our family cottage to see if we could figure it out together. It took us a couple of weeks, on and off, but the end product turned out really nicely, if I do say so myself. The cradle was supported by two dowels so that it could rock back and forth, and the first time I lowered Bruce into it, I was suddenly filled with fear that the whole thing would collapse under his body weight. *Please, Jesus*, I thought, *stay together*. Fortunately, the structure held, and Bruce took to it right away. Anne and I placed it next to our bed, and Bruce slept there peacefully for the next few months.

The plan, going forward, was that Anne would take three or four months off to be with Bruce, and then go back to work. We both had good jobs—me as a broadcaster, and she as the marketing director for a couple of shopping centres around Winnipeg—so we weren't under a lot of financial pressure, but the thought of living on just one income still seemed risky. Plus, Anne liked her career and didn't want to leave it behind just like that.

So she put an ad in the newspaper and found a family in nearby Linden Woods to look after Bruce while we were both at work. Rana and Purvis Shere were a lovely couple who did a great job taking care of him. Each morning, I would drop Bruce off at the Sheres' place, and then Anne would pick him up at the end of the workday. It was a busy arrangement, especially with me being on the road so much, but Bruce loved the attention from the Sheres and we found a way to make it work. They had a couple of kids of their own, one of whom was still a toddler, and they all loved spending time together.

But like I mentioned, Bruce was a good baby and an even better sleeper, almost *too* good of a sleeper. When you factor in all of those unconscious hours, plus the full eight-hour workday and commute, Anne found she hardly got any quality time with her son. She'd have about half an hour with Bruce each morning, and then another

hour or so after she got back home in the evening. But that wasn't enough.

One night we were eating dinner together after Bruce was in bed, and she seemed equal parts sad and frustrated. Finally, she said, "This isn't working for me." It was clear something had to change: she knew it, I knew it, and, it turned out, even her boss at work knew it. And so, just three months into her return to work, Anne quit for good. From that point onwards, full-time motherhood took over.

Soon enough, our house got busier, too. Anne and I were expecting our second child. By then Bruce was just over two years old—which was, as it turned out, the time things started to change for him. Our calm, content newborn quickly became a very difficult toddler. And it took Anne and me a long time to figure out why, and what, if anything, we could do to help him.

Compared to the marathon labour that accompanied Bruce's birth, the arrival of our second son, Darcy, was a walk in the park. In fact, it started with one.

The fall of 1987, I was hosting CFL games on CBC, and that particular Saturday I was away covering a game in Ottawa. When I got home on Sunday afternoon, Anne was there at the front door, saying, "I think I need to go to the hospital."

But because Bruce had needed nearly twenty-four hours to finally be born, I figured we still had plenty of time. So I took Bruce, who was by now a toddler, on a walk to a nice park and playground near our house. I'd missed him while I was away, and we had a good time together, especially since I knew our lives were about to change again—and soon.

When we came back, Anne was there again, and this time she was more adamant: "Okay, time to go. Now."

Fair enough.

We went and got admitted to the hospital, and once Anne was settled in a bed, I popped out to the Coke machine to get a drink, again trying to pace myself as I expected the labour to be long like with Bruce. I hadn't even gotten my change back when a nurse came out and said, "Uh, Mr. Oake, you better get in here right now."

By the time I hurried back into the room, Darcy was already born. It was such a quick labour, it was almost as if he'd come out with rugburns on his face. Unfortunately, I could see right away that Darcy was born with the dreaded Oake gene, which meant he already had quite possibly the biggest head known to mankind. Thankfully, Anne survived the ordeal with no complications and Darcy spent the better part of his life growing into that head, only catching up now that he's in his thirties.

The other complication with Darcy's birth was that he came out with jaundice. The doctor told us he needed to go into an incubator for a couple of days, which was not news Anne and I wanted to hear. The doctors decided that she should stay at the hospital to be near him while I went home to take care of Bruce.

Back at home, I quickly realized that taking care of a toddler was a full-time job, and thanked my lucky stars once more that I had someone as capable as Anne in charge most of the time. But I did my best to keep the house running as it usually did. When I told Bruce it was time go to the hospital to visit them, he got excited and said,

"We're going to Mommy's house!" I'm still not sure what he meant by that. Along the way I stopped and got takeout from one of Anne's favourite restaurants, so we could have dinner together.

At first, I don't think Bruce was quite sure what to think about suddenly being an older brother. But then again, their first meeting was a bit unusual—Darcy was still inside the incubator, and was wearing these giant hospital-issued goggles to protect his eyes from the bright lights used to treat his jaundice.

It all seemed surreal to me. But Bruce just stood there, taking it all in.

Most people would agree that one kid is a lot of work. But it's important to know that two kids aren't two times the work—it feels like it's about five. Darcy was a pretty good baby, all things considered, but he required more attention to get to sleep and stay asleep than Bruce had. He had to be rocked to sleep every single night. I remember sitting in the rocking chair with him, thinking, *Okay, we've been motionless for about half an hour. That must be long enough.* Well, my arms may have been asleep, but apparently Darcy wasn't. As soon as I'd get up, he would start yelping and I'd have to start the whole routine all over again.

Once again, the bulk of the parenting workload fell onto Anne's shoulders, because my career was carrying on more or less uninterrupted.

My main gig was still doing the local sports for the CBC's supper-hour news in Winnipeg, and a lot of the times I did the late broadcast, too, because back then we had early and late local-news packages. I realize this sounds like ancient history now, since highlights are so easily accessible these days. (Sometimes it feels like sports highlights are running twenty-four hours a day.) But back then, in the '80s, it was still considered an important part of the overall broadcast.

Basically, it was my job to find a new local sports story every day. This meant running around and shooting interviews with players or staff from the Bombers, the Jets, an amateur team, or something else entirely. Generally I would get to work at 10 or 11 a.m. and try to think up a story that hadn't already been done. Then I'd have to find a cameraman to go out with me to shoot it, and then we'd both hustle back to the station to edit it in time for the broadcast.

It's not much of an exaggeration, however, to say that I was the most disorganized sportscaster in the history of the business. Let's say the sports segment was scheduled to come on the air at 6:20 p.m. It wasn't unusual for me to be running downstairs to the edit suites at 5:55 with my arms full of tapes—every tape except the one I needed. I'd quickly record a voice-over that I'd scrawled on the back of a napkin, then hand it over to the editor whose job it was to dig up the footage that would make the story make sense. Then I'd rush back upstairs, put on a shirt and tie, plop myself down in front of the cameras, and pray that the story would roll when I called for it. Somehow, it always did. But, my God, the number of times the editors would plead to me, "You've got to get more organized here."

I took those complaints to heart. Really, I did. But then two days later I'd find myself doing the same thing all over again. In all honesty, the job should have been a lot easier than I made it. And if any of my old editors are reading this, I expect they're nodding right now.

The pace at home, however, was much different, mostly because Anne ran the house, and she kept everything calm and organized. She knew the time of every doctor's appointment and the location of every swimming lesson. That was just part of her personality in general. She didn't leave a lot to chance. For me, Anne's level of care was such a gift, because it allowed me to fully concentrate on my work while I was away, and to feel like we could handle anything when we were together.

I often think back on that period in our lives and how I lucky I was—how Anne always put my career first, even with two small children in the house. In my line of work, with its odd hours and constant travel requirements, an awful lot of marriages fall apart because the two spouses aren't on the same wavelength. When one half is away as much as I was, you better be secure—and thankful—in the knowledge that your partner can handle whatever comes up. And Anne could.

As usual, I was away from home more than I would've liked, travelling across the country—and sometimes even further than that. In the summer of 1988, I was sent to Seoul to cover another Olympic Games for the CBC. Back then it was standard to send a few commentators and producers out early—three or four weeks before the Games actually started—to put together feature stories in advance. So I was gone for around seven weeks in total, at a time when Darcy was still an infant, and Bruce was just turning three.

This was long before cell phones, of course, at a time when long-distance calls were still ridiculously expensive. The arrangement with the CBC was that they would pay for two calls home each week. Well, that obviously wasn't going to be enough for me. Whenever I found myself back at the broadcast centre with a minute to spare, I'd grab the nearest phone and dial Winnipeg. This way the call couldn't be billed to me directly, and it became a running joke among my colleagues, who would routinely catch me in the act. Our business manager gave me shit about it, too, but not that much, because she knew I had small kids.

Those phone calls were important to me, but they didn't always leave me feeling any less homesick. One day I called home from a pay phone in the lobby of my hotel, and Anne said, "Hang on a second, Bruce wants to talk." He was still figuring out how to put sentences together, and the only thing he said when he came to the phone that day was "Daddy come home," over and over again. Oh boy, was that tough to hear. I felt tears spring to my eyes immediately. And the Games hadn't even started yet!

Darcy and Bruce had separate rooms from the beginning, located right across the hall from each other. This was by design: in the weeks before Bruce was born, Anne and I had bought a house together large enough to raise a family in. It was certainly a heck of a lot different than how I'd grown up in Nova Scotia, with five kids, two parents, and one grandfather constantly bumping elbows. I was proud to know that my kids would have a bit more breathing room.

We were also fortunate to be able to travel quite a lot with the kids when they were younger. We tried to make it out to my parents' place back in Amherst, Nova Scotia, twice a year—once at Christmas and once in the summer. The kids loved going to Grammy and Grandpa's, obviously, because they were always spoiled rotten there. Walt was well known for his sweet tooth, and he gave the kids unlimited access to the special fridge he kept full of chocolate bars. We also made family trips to Hawaii, Mexico, and Disneyland a couple

of times. The funny thing was, I'd built up so many Aeroplan points through work that the battle cry from the kids soon became that they weren't going anywhere unless they could fly business class.

It's a small thing, of course, but I always saw these flight upgrades as one of the benefits of working and being away so much. If I could do that for my kids, and bring a smile to their faces, why wouldn't I?

It was on one of those trips to Disneyland where I first remember noticing something unusual in Bruce's behaviour. He'd always been particular about certain things, but now he outright refused to go on certain rides. At first, it looked like a normal enough fear—he seemed to be bothered by the rides that went too high in the air—but there was something in his stubbornness that surprised me. Stranger still, I could tell he was trying to mask his fear, as if he didn't want anyone else to know that this was the real thing holding him back. In the moment, I thought he was just being difficult, and tried to force the issue. But Bruce dug his heels in even more fervently, and all four of us ended up leaving the park entirely and spending the rest of the day at the pool at our hotel.

We were soon to discover that Bruce's anxieties were only beginning, and that the list of things and situations that bothered him in this way would only continue to grow.

At Bruce's kindergarten Christmas concert, he was cast as the Snow King—a lead role that meant he had to speak a few lines into a shared microphone. Anne and I sat in the crowd, proud that he'd been given such an important role. After his part was done, however, Bruce realized that even when someone else was speaking, if he made a noise, then everyone would hear it. So he just started banging on the mic. The chaos that ensued made a bunch of the other parents start to laugh, but Anne and I just sat there, mortified. All we could think was, *Oh my God, he's ruining it. He's ruining it for everybody.*

Looking back on it, of course, it wasn't that big of a deal. But we were so concerned with trying to get Bruce to behave like the other kids, and whenever he couldn't do it, we took the failure personally.

Anne ended up volunteering at the school whenever there was a function or a field trip, partly to help, but partly to make sure Bruce toed the line. He managed to do okay academically, thanks to the help of his teachers, most of whom were kind and compassionate and always did their best to help him fit in. But there's no question he found school challenging, and took his share of discipline as a result. He heard the word "stop" so often, it should have been on his birth certificate.

Bruce had an odd habit of having to be the last person to say goodbye when he left the house for school. If, for whatever reason, we said goodbye after he did, he'd bang on the door and insist on redoing the ending, this time on his terms. I'm sorry to say it, but sometimes Anne I would kill ourselves laughing over this. "Uh-oh," we'd say to each other, "here comes the knock!"

He also struggled with going to elementary school, even though it was just up the street from our house. Every day he would come home for lunch with Anne, and every day he would claim he had a stomachache and couldn't go back. It was a constant challenge for her, trying to find new ways of convincing him, and oftentimes they ended up making a deal where if Bruce was a good boy and went back to school, there'd be a treat waiting for him at home afterwards. Other days, he required different negotiating tactics. Anne winded up using just about every trick in the parenting handbook.

Individually, these episodes of Bruce's seemed like harmless quirks, but they were a sign of things to come. Anne and I couldn't see the pattern for what it was yet, because the pattern was still establishing itself, and we were just trying to figure out this thing called parenting as best we could.

When Bruce was five or six, Anne took him to see the Winnipeg Symphony's performance of *The Nutcracker* at Christmas. He was excited to get all dressed up and have a special evening with his mom. But it turned out this was a slightly different version of the story than usual, and for some reason, the mice—Bruce's favourite characters—weren't in this one. It took Bruce a while to figure out what was going on, but once he did, he started angrily tugging at Anne's dress. "Where are the mice?" he asked her. "Where are the mice?"

"This one's a little different, Bruce," Anne said.

She was trying to reassure him, but it didn't work. Bruce started yelling, right in the middle of the crowd, "You lied to me! You're a liar!"

It was such an intense outburst that Anne really got upset by it, and when they got back home she went straight to bed. Mostly, though, we were just confused. It made sense for a kid to be upset about missing their favourite characters in a show. But Bruce's level of outrage was unsettling—it was as if Anne herself had called ahead and specifically asked the symphony to keep the mice out. He was so angry, and so angry *at her*. At times like that, Anne and I had to admit that Bruce had fundamentally changed from those first two years, when pretty much everything went smoothly.

For years, after the kids were asleep, it was common for Anne and me to stay up late and try to figure out what we were going to do about Bruce. We knew we needed help, on some level, which is why we went to Bruce's paediatrician, Dr. Neil Margolis, to see what might be going on beneath the surface.

Dr. Margolis had already tried to help us figure out some of Bruce's earliest quirks, including a recurring tic where he would repeatedly wipe his mouth with the sleeve of his shirt to the point of rubbing his lips raw. Anne and I had a series of phone calls, and even one lunch, with Dr. Margolis to try to figure out what, exactly, was going on, and what we might try to fix it. Dr. Margolis suggested things like pinning Bruce's sleeve to his pyjama top, or tying a towel around it so he physically couldn't do the wiping action. That evening we tried it out, but it seemed so cruel that we quickly gave it up. It also didn't seem like it was getting to the root of the problem. Sure enough, soon afterwards that tic subsided on its own, only to be replaced by a totally different one.

Of course, it's not that Bruce was *always* difficult. In a lot of ways, he was your typical kid, full of energy and wanting to make us happy.

He liked being read to, and he liked watching TV. *Sharon, Lois & Bram* was always his go-to show. Whenever he was upset, we'd plunk him down in front of that and he was good to go. It was almost like a sedative. Bruce and Darcy also both adored those old Raffi singalong tapes. We have a cottage in Whiteshell Provincial Park that we'd go to in the summertime, and the drive was just under two hours by car, an ideal distance in that it was just far enough away that we could get there without an argument breaking out. And "Down by the Bay" would be playing in the car just about the entire way, there and back. Those Raffi songs are still stuck in my head to this day.

He also loved sports, especially basketball and boxing. I took Bruce for skating lessons when he was little, but hockey—what his father would end up making his livelihood on—never appealed to him, in part because he never had the attention span to sit down and watch an entire game on TV. Once, the two of us were outside playing street hockey. Like any Canadian dad, I was giving him all of this advice: how to hold the stick, how to shoot, and so on. A litany of directions. Until Bruce, who always seemed to want to argue, even if was a topic he knew nothing about, decided he'd had enough.

"If you know so much about hockey," he yelled, "then you should be playing it, not just talking about it!"

(In this case, he may have had a point. Even at the age of four, he'd already figured out his father was nothing more than a professional gasbag.)

Bruce did have some funny reactions to my being on television every evening. His eyes would always light up whenever I came on the screen, and I remember one day in particular when he was younger, he got totally confused when he saw me suddenly appear during a segment that had been prerecorded. I was sitting next to him on the couch, and I asked him, "Who's that, Bruce?"

He took a second to assess the situation, then answered confidently, "That's the old Daddy."

"Oh. Well, then, who am I?"

He smiled. "You're the new Daddy."

I have no idea where on earth he came up with that. But then again, that kid always had an answer for everything.

• • •

In my opinion, there's no better case study for the eternal question of nature versus nurture than having two kids, who are roughly the same age, and raised in the exact same way—and who yet wind up with completely different temperaments.

Anne and I would watch Darcy and Bruce play together, and think: Why is one kid so defiant, yet the other will go along with anything? Darcy had become a kid who was always easy-going and even-keeled. At our cottage, for instance, he was so excited to attend what he called "party night" with our neighbours, Ray and Brenda Ford, and their daughter, Jennifer. Whereas Bruce was precisely the opposite: cautious, on edge, and prone to meltdowns.

Case in point was the day Bruce first rode a two-wheeled bicycle. He'd used training wheels for a while, but now it was time to take them off. Once again, I was trying to help him ease into it, and Bruce kept yelling, "Let me go, I can do it! Let me go!" But as soon as I'd let him go, he'd immediately fall over and get incredibly frustrated. Meanwhile, Darcy, two full years younger, asked, "Can I try?"—and then he hopped on the same bike and pretty much rode it all the way home. It wasn't a question of ability so much as personality. Darcy was calm enough to figure things out, whereas Bruce was so insistent on acting like he already knew everything that you couldn't actually teach him a thing. The contrast between their temperaments was obvious even at a distance.

As Bruce went through elementary school, he did his best to hide these behaviours and worries from the rest of the world. Bruce would never just admit he couldn't bring himself to do something. Instead, he'd get sullen and pretend he wasn't interested. So Anne and I had

to become amateur detectives, trying to read between the lines and decipher what was really going on with our eldest child.

Bruce was also extremely determined and once he put his mind to something, he was difficult to dissuade—especially when it came to things that were forbidden. When Bruce was eight, Anne and I went away to the Grey Cup, and my mom came out to take care of him and his brother. The three of them walked over to our local video store, where Bruce promptly took off straight into the adult section. He brought back some X-rated movie and Grammy—horrified, I'm sure—gently told him he shouldn't be looking at things like that.

"No, no," Bruce told her, "I talked to my parents before they left and they said I could watch this!"

We knew we needed help, and so we dragged Bruce to numerous specialists, in the hopes that someone could help us figure out what, exactly, was going on with him. To his credit, Bruce always agreed to come and never complained about it—maybe on some level he wanted some peace of mind, too. The child psychiatrist we took him to told us it was important to set boundaries, and not to be afraid to stick to our guns. We tried to follow his advice, but it was always a battle, and as often as not, we ended up giving in.

What made Bruce's emerging behaviours even more difficult to grapple with was the fact that we all knew he never set out to upset us. I maintain that he always wanted to make Anne and me happy, right up until the day he died. But there were other factors—internal and external—that got in the way.

It took some time to put a name on what was going on with Bruce. When he was around seven years old, I told a good friend of mine from work about Bruce's oppositional behaviour and he suggested that we take Bruce in to see a clinical psychologist he knew named Seymour Opochinsky.

Dr. Opochinsky was a lovely old gentleman who welcomed Bruce, Anne, and me into his office. First he sat down with Bruce one on one. Then he sent him off to play in an area that was out of earshot, and brought Anne and me in together to discuss what he'd observed.

He told us, "Look, Bruce is clearly a very smart kid, but he's showing signs of ADD." (This was later upgraded to ADHD.) Dr. Opochinsky told us he'd also noticed Bruce's incredible levels of determination, which we'd seen up close and personal at home. But, he suggested, it was difficult for Bruce to use that intelligence and that focus because of his difficulties focusing on tasks in front of him.

We then discussed a series of common markers for ADD/ADHD, and it was obvious to both Anne and me that Bruce had almost all of them.

Persistent inattention? Check.

Incessant talking? Check.

Frequent fidgeting? Check.

Emotional outbursts? Interrupts others? Self-focused? Trouble waiting his turn? Careless mistakes?

Check, check, check, check, check.

For Anne and me, hearing that diagnosis made us both relieved and concerned. On the one hand, now there seemed to be an overarching reason for his behaviour, but on the other hand, all parents want to believe that their kids are perfect. Subconsciously, we wanted Dr. Opochinsky to tell us this was all just a phase and that it would go away on its own. But now it was sinking in that this was something Bruce would, in all likelihood, have to deal with for the long term.

Around this same time, I got to talking with another friend at work whose son had recently been diagnosed with Tourette's. I was telling him a story about Bruce one day and he cut me off: "That sounds an awful lot like Tourette's to me." He suggested we make an appointment with his son's psychiatrist—and sure enough, they diagnosed Bruce with Tourette's, too.

This wasn't totally a surprise, given another tic Bruce had developed, where he would quickly shake his head three or four times. This didn't seem to Anne or me like a serious problem, since Bruce didn't have the coprolalia symptom, where you suddenly and involuntarily scream obscenities. But as we only gradually figured out, it took a lot of inner strength on Bruce's part to keep even his milder tics under control. He would do things like curl his toes or ball his hands up into fists, and that would reduce the urge to do the compulsive action.

With this second diagnosis, Bruce was then enrolled in a specialized Tourette's clinic. That's where medication was first presented as an option. This was obviously a bigger step in terms of treatment, but Anne and I were willing to try anything in the hopes of seeing an improvement in Bruce's behaviour. At the same time, the word *Tourette's* was scarier to me, both because of how significant its effects can be, and because there's a real stigma attached to it. But the clonidine Bruce was prescribed had side effects—suddenly he had a lot less energy, and he also gained weight. He ended up staying with the clinic for a couple of years, until the end of grade six, but I'm not sure it was much help to him.

Honestly, the whole situation was so hard for Anne and me to understand. We were getting a crash-course education, but in those early days I found myself saying reductive, unhelpful things to Bruce like, "Just stop doing that. You don't need to do that." It took a long time for Anne and me to understand the underlying conditions that made those external symptoms pop up.

In the meantime, there were a lot of battles in our house. One of the worst ones took place on a Friday afternoon, just as we were about to leave for the cottage. I was finishing up packing everything into the family Buick and Darcy climbed into the backseat—the seat that Bruce wanted. Right away, they started arguing. To end things, I told Darcy to give Bruce the seat, but that wasn't enough. Bruce was still fuming. Before I knew it, we were all shouting at each other in the driveway.

Now, we never spanked our kids. There was only one time I ever laid a finger on them—and it was that afternoon. Bruce was being so unreasonable that I'd finally had it. I hauled him out of the car and gave him a small but meaningful whack on the butt. Bruce knew right away that this was new territory. He was so shocked that he looked across the street to where our neighbours happened to be standing, and yelled to them, "My dad hit me!"

(For what it's worth, these neighbours just looked back at him, like, *Buddy, you're lucky you're not on this side of the street, because you would have got it a lot worse from us!*)

I then told Bruce the trip was off, and he had to go to his room. My intention was to send him up there for a long time, so he could think about what he'd done. But before long I'd calmed down enough to realize that I needed to put things right first. I knocked on Bruce's door and told him, "Daddy is so sorry. I shouldn't have done that." I was hoping this apology would induce Bruce to acknowledge his own misbehaviour, but he didn't say anything. Instead, he ran right past me and went downstairs to Anne, who was in the kitchen, and said brightly, "Dad just apologized, are you going to?"

It was exhausting.

Fighting those same battles over and over again wore us down over the years. There was definitely a lot of frustration. But everything Anne and I ever did came from a place of love, and wanting to help him, because it was so hard for us to watch our son as he struggled. Sometimes I would think back to Bruce when he was an infant, sleeping peacefully in that homemade cradle for twelve hours at a time, and wonder what had gone wrong. How had he turned into this child who was now full of so much anger and stubbornness? What kind of switch had been flipped inside of him—and how could I flip it back?

We were willing to do anything to get Bruce to unwind a bit and make our household more peaceful. But nothing seemed to work. Invoking consequences, for instance, was a nonstarter, because we could tell those things literally never crossed Bruce's mind when he was in the middle of doing something. In the moment, he would simply do whatever he felt like doing, consequences be damned. Whenever we tried to bring up those consequences to him after the fact, it only ever seemed to lead to another argument.

As things got more difficult for Bruce, I used to ask myself a lot of *what if* questions. What if I'd had a different career? What if I'd been around more? Would that have helped him? I'm not sure what, exactly, might have been different. Maybe I'd have been able to do something, or maybe just my being there would have helped him in some small way. I don't know. But if you have any compassion as a human being, it's impossible not to think about those things.

Whenever I start thinking about Bruce's life, it's easy to look past the happy memories and zero in on the difficult ones. But not every day was a catastrophe. We had so many good memories as well—Bruce and I together, Bruce with his mom or his younger brother, or all four of us as a family. I remember taking the boys to their swimming lessons, and our family outings to the movies (how could I forget the time we happened to go see *There's Something About Mary*, after which Anne had to come up with a delicate explanation for the infamous "hair gel" scene?). We also had a great time going out to eat together, especially at Homers, a longstanding Greek restaurant just down the street from the CBC building. I used to take the boys there all the time for dinner, and they loved running around in the aisles and joking around with George, the owner, who would always drop by our table to say hello.

But I often wonder, now knowing that Bruce was struggling with ADHD, how he got through those days. His mind worked liked a weedwhacker. Every once in a while, it would land on something he was interested in, but otherwise, good luck getting him to slow down. Try as he might, he just couldn't stop and focus on anything that didn't automatically grab his attention. And most things in school didn't. Once, as a teenager, he and Anne drove past his old elementary school, and he said to her, "I remember those days. I never knew where to go or what to do, and people were always yelling at me."

Three

In the Ring

The peak of Bruce's athletic career came at age fifteen, when he stepped into the boxing ring one evening and proceeded to beat the shit out of an old guy who didn't see it coming: me.

While Bruce was never an extraordinarily talented athlete, that dogged determination that made our household so tumultuous did serve him well in the sporting world. This was especially true when it came to boxing—a sport that first got his attention when he saw me on TV, covering it for the Summer Olympics in Atlanta in 1996 and again in Sydney four years later. Bruce was eleven during the Atlanta games, and he took my interest in the sport as a sign. Despite our arguments, he loved Anne and me dearly and always wanted to please us. I think he saw me covering boxing and thought, *Dad will like it if I try that.*

In reality, it was a bit more complicated. When Bruce started bugging us to sign him up for boxing classes, Anne and I dragged our heels for weeks. Because what parent wants to see their kid get hit in the head? Boxers do wear certain pieces of safety equipment and headgear, of course, but there's an ongoing debate about how effective any of that stuff is in the long run. Ultimately it didn't matter, because Bruce could not be dissuaded. It was clearly only a matter of time until we gave in. So I took him over to the Crescentwood Boxing Club, not far from our house, and signed him up.

Soon enough, Bruce was thrown into a number of amateur fights, and to Anne's and my surprise, he was pretty good. Certainly nobody in my family would've ever had the courage to put on the gloves unless they had three or four shots of rye under their belt first. But Bruce took to the sport quickly. By the time he was a teenager, it wasn't uncommon for him to get into a van with his clubmates and drive to some small town in northern Minnesota, where he'd fight someone two years older than him. Sometimes he won, sometimes he didn't. And no matter where he went, he brought his baby blanket—a light green item that had been part of his first sheet set, long since threadbare—along with him as a good-luck charm.

I was really happy to see him dedicate himself to something and do well at it—which he did, for a couple of years. He trained hard and had some success. As a parent, you always take pride in your kid finding an activity that speaks to them. Of course, it didn't hurt that I was already a fan of what's sometimes called the manly art of self-defence, so it was also just fun to watch him in action. I could tell my support meant something to him, too. There was more than one fight where, at the end of a particularly good round, he first looked out at

me in the crowd rather than to his trainer, who was there in the ring with him.

At the same time, boxing held an appeal for Bruce because it allowed him to tap into a tough-guy lifestyle that he found himself increasingly attracted to. To him, boxing was cool *because* it was dangerous, or had the potential to be. It wasn't a mainstream sport. It was kind of on the margins, and he liked that about it.

No matter the motivation, he won a bunch of fights, and showed improvement in the ring. That's when he decided, one evening after training, to see if he could beat up his old man.

It wasn't the first time he'd asked me to get in the ring with him. I love boxing, as I've said, and I'd often hang around and watch his training sessions just for fun. And as he got stronger and more confident in his abilities, Bruce had asked me probably five or six times to get in there with him. I knew there was nothing to be gained by doing it, so I always refused. But on this one particular evening, Darcy and I had gone to pick him up from Crescentwood, and he was the last person in there. He was getting ready to lock up and turn off the lights, when he turned to me and challenged me again.

"C'mon, Dad," he said with a smile. "Let's see what you got."

To this day, I'm not sure why I agreed. I suppose one reason is that there was no one else around to see the outcome besides Darcy. For another, I was still the parent, after all. Who knew? Maybe I'd surprise myself with some reserve of hidden talent that even I didn't know was there.

I got in the ring, in my socked feet, and put some gloves on.

The next twenty seconds are a blur.

All I remember is being doubled over against the corner turnbuckle as my teenaged son mercilessly rained shots down on my kidneys. There was only one thought in my mind: *I really hope I'm not gonna be pissing blood after this.*

Bruce wasn't trying to hurt me, of course. He was in his element, and he wanted to show me what he could do and what he'd been training towards. Let's just say it didn't take him long to prove his point. As I lay there in a helpless ball, Bruce looked down at me and made one final show of theatrical disgust. He held his hand up, waved at me dismissively, and walked away. Darcy, sitting ringside, aghast at his father's performance but secretly loving every second of the tilt.

On the drive back home, I was feeling sorry for myself. But Bruce, in the passenger seat, was on top of the world, and decided to add a bit of salt to the wound by saying, as we pulled into the driveway, "You know, Dad, I just realized that if a criminal ever broke into our house, I'd have to save us, because you sure couldn't."

To cover my wounded pride, I made up some horseshit about how that's actually not true, because boxing was a totally different situation than real life. But I was only trying to convince myself. The fact was that Bruce had been training for a long time, and he'd gotten a lot faster and stronger than I was. To any observer, it was obvious: I never should have gotten into that ring with him.

Thanks to his hard work, by the time he was in grade 12, Bruce made the provincial team for his age group and was selected to compete at that year's Canada Games, which were being held in Bathurst, New Brunswick. When he told us, Anne, Darcy, and I were overjoyed. It was a really impressive accomplishment—especially because it was the result of hard work above all else. What Bruce lacked in natural athletic ability, he had made up for in sheer determination.

(I remember, for another example, taking the boys golfing together at Falcon Lake once: Darcy had a natural, graceful swing, whereas Bruce was channelling his inner Happy Gilmore, sledgehammering the ball into submission.)

At the Canada Games, Bruce's first fight was against a kid from Newfoundland. I wasn't able to be there, unfortunately, but my parents drove up to watch, and my father told me afterwards that Bruce pretty much dominated the kid. Bruce wasn't an elegant fighter, but he was tough, and his straight-ahead fighting approach worked in his favour.

For his second match, Bruce was up against a brute from Quebec. We all knew it was going to be tough, because those Quebecois fighters were all good. But this time, Darcy and I were able to fly out in time to see it and cheer Bruce on in person.

I could tell Bruce was nervous because he spent a lot of time running on the spot, trying to get his nerves under control. But he managed to more or less hold his own for the first round, and as soon as the bell rang, he looked straight over at me in the crowd. We made eye contact, and I tried to convey without words that I believed in him. It was a funny moment, because Bruce was so focused on getting my approval that his trainer had to give him a tap on the forehead, as if to say, *Hey, eyes over here.*

In the second round, however, things went sideways in a hurry. Bruce was clearly overmatched, and before long the fight got stopped. He lost by TKO.

Bruce was then taken to a medical room for assessment, and I went back there to see him. He was really upset. Not only had he desperately wanted to win the match for its own sake—he also wanted to do it with me and the rest of the family in the crowd, cheering him on. But he felt he'd let himself down, even if on paper he was clearly the underdog.

In a way, though, I think that twenty-second fight against me was just as important to him as anything he did in Bathurst. At the very least, it answered a fundamental question in his mind. After all, most kids *think* they could take their old man in a fight, but they never get to find out the answer for sure. Bruce did.

As Bruce got older, he was discovering who he wanted to be, and what he wanted to get out of life—and that meant independence.

Our house has three bedrooms on the top floor, and from the time the kids were born, that's where we all slept. But by the time Bruce was in grade 6 or 7, he set his sights on moving down to our basement. The basement had been finished pretty much since we moved in, and there was space for a bedroom down there. Anne and I told him he was too young to be that far away from the rest of us, but, once again, in came that dogged determination. Bruce argued that if we were going to let him move down there someday, what difference did it make if it was now or in a year? Every day he brought it up, again and again and again and *again*. Sigh. Down to the basement he went.

The other room on that floor was my home office—or, at least, that's what it was intended to be. We had a big desktop computer set up down there, which I used for a time. But as soon as laptops came along, I was too lazy to haul my ass all the way down to the basement

For the Love *of a* Son

every morning. Which left Bruce with easy access to a computer that nobody else ever used.

One day, Anne came down to the basement when Bruce wasn't home and saw there was a bunch of porn left open on the desktop. This kicked off a great investigation in our house to determine who did it. Of course, we all knew it was Bruce. It was clear as day, but Anne and I wanted him to come clean on his own. We called him up to the dinner table and said to him, "Look, if you did it, just admit it."

Bruce denied it. By this point in his life, he had become a gifted liar, feigning innocence with such conviction that it made you second-guess even the most obvious facts. But in this case, Anne and I were so certain that it was him that we kept confronting him about it over the next couple of days.

Finally, he realized we weren't giving up. "Okay," he said carefully, "I'm not saying it *was* me, but . . . if it was, what kind of trouble would I be looking at?"

That computer is also where Bruce nurtured his other big hobby, after boxing: music, specifically hip-hop and rap. He'd loved rap from an early age. One of his first favourite songs was MC Hammer's "U Can't Touch This," and he used to sit in his room listening to it on an endless loop, memorizing every line and every rhythm.

Sometimes, though, there was a bit of a disconnect. There was a lyric he once heard where the rapper talked about having a thousand "brothers" in jail. I remember Bruce, confused, asking me how that could possibly be true. He hadn't grasped yet that the rapper didn't mean his literal brothers. The slang had gone right over his head.

While Bruce loved hip-hop, Darcy could have cared less. When Christmas 1996 rolled around, Bruce, who was eleven, and Darcy, who was nine, asked for CDs in their stockings. Darcy was so excited to get the debut album from Donna Lewis, whose pop song "I Love You Always Forever" was unavoidable that entire year. Bruce, meanwhile, got the latest by Snoop Dogg. It was quite a contrast.

(In fairness, I should point out that poor Darcy eventually came around to hip-hop, and even helped me out of a jam during the Stanley Cup Finals in 2007. Ottawa was playing Anaheim, and one day our producer told me that the aforementioned Snoop Dogg himself was going to be at the game that night—and that I had to interview him. I called Darcy in a panic and asked for ideas on what to say. Without hesitation, Darcy said, "Write this down: 'I'm with the Doggfather, D-O-double-gizzy. Big ups on this crunk planet. What's crackellating, nephew?'"

I paused and said, "Is that English?"

He assured me that it was, and coached me on how to say it—apparently, my initial attempt was so bad that Darcy warned me that Snoop might kick the shit out of me if I didn't improve, and fast. I must've worked on that lyric for an hour in the mirror. But during the broadcast, Snoop, who is a big California hockey fan, seemed impressed. At the very least, I escaped without another beating.)

Anne and I were worried about Bruce's obsession with rap, especially once his taste moved on from artists like MC Hammer to more intense rappers like Biggie Smalls and Tupac, who wrote about gang violence and drugs, among other things. But then again, how do parents ever govern the kind of music their kids like? Is it ever successful? You can just ban it from the house, I suppose, or turn it off whenever you happen to come across it. But then Bruce would just head off downstairs to his bedroom and the computer, and good luck.

To her credit, Anne was more understanding about things than I was, and recognized that listening to edgy music was just what teenagers did—no different, really, than how kids of our generation had turned to bands like the Beatles while our parents couldn't get over their haircuts. So yes, rap seemed alienating and crass to us. That was the whole point.

Whereas I tended to have a more typical knee-jerk reaction, barking things like, "This music will never stand the test of time—mark my words, nobody will be listening to 'In da Club' forty years from now!"

To which Anne would reply, "Don't be such a fuddy-duddy asshole."

She was right.

Still, Bruce fell for rap so hard and so quickly that it became a joke in the family. Sometimes we'd all be sitting watching a movie together, and there'd be a scene where gang members drove around in their fancy chopped-up cars. Darcy would poke Bruce and say, "Hey, look, it's your dream come true."

Harry Neale, my former colleague at *Hockey Night in Canada*, used to say about hip-hop, "That's not music—that's a guy making a speech." At first, that's how I looked at it, too. But as Bruce got more interested, I'll admit I came around a bit to the energy and charisma shown by some of those artists. There may or may not be a couple of Ludacris songs on my phone right now.

Later on, in high school, Bruce took the obvious next step and started writing his own rap lyrics. This endeavour came with a predictable learning curve, and Anne and I used to kill ourselves laughing when we read some of what he'd come up with. One memorable early lyric of Bruce's went, "I was born in the gritty, and I'll die in the gritty." We said to him, "You should change that to something a little more realistic—like, 'I was born in a comfortable home in the south end of Winnipeg, and I'll die in a comfortable home in the south end of Winnipeg.'" But I guess that doesn't roll off the tongue quite so nicely.

One night, when he was in grade 12, Bruce asked me if he could go to the nearby University of Manitoba campus for a rap battle. Anne was out of town, so I said yes, but told him he had to be home by 10 o'clock. He agreed, and took off. But when 10 p.m. came around, he wasn't back yet. At 11 p.m., same thing. I stayed up waiting for him, my mind swinging from worry to anger and back again. By the time midnight rolled around, I was standing at our front door, peering out the window and dreaming up all kinds of punishment. Finally, Bruce showed up. He casually came through the doorway and, to my surprise, waved five crisp $100 bills in my face.

"Hey, Dad, look!" he said. "I won the whole thing!"

I smiled, my irritation instantly replaced by relief, and said, "Well, if you're going to come home late, that's the way to do it. Now go to bed."

What I came to learn was that the realism of Bruce's rap lyrics was never the point—rap offered a kind of escapism from his actual life, which was privileged and safe. To him, the world of hip-hop represented a lifestyle that was both forbidden and more authentic. It was a lifestyle that he idolized, and one that, eventually, he tried to embody.

• • •

At around the same time he started getting into boxing and rapping, Bruce started attending a new school called Linden Christian. The move was our idea. We thought—and Bruce agreed—that socially it wasn't working for him at his previous school. He wasn't happy there, and some of the other kids picked up on his sensitivity and took advantage of it. One day, for instance, word got around the schoolyard that Anne's mother had just died, and before long one of Bruce's classmates started making a bunch of dead-grandmother jokes to him. He got so upset that it led to a fight—which, of course, only egged the other kids on. As parents, Anne and I felt awful for him, and just wanted Bruce to have a way to feel better about himself.

Sure enough, Bruce blossomed in his new surroundings. He quickly grew more self-assured and more confident. Over time he became one of the biggest personalities in his class—which also meant he had detention pretty much every day. I would hear more or less constant stories about Bruce getting in trouble for talking in class and not paying attention. He also wore T-shirts bearing aggressive slogans from his favourite WWF wrestlers, and was a vocal proponent of the Pen15 Club (if you've never heard of it, and someone asks you to join while waving around a Sharpie, run the other direction).

Unfortunately, his grades didn't rise along with his self-esteem. As hard as we tried, I don't think Anne or I ever once saw Bruce open a book at home. But he was smart enough to get by at school, and that's what he did. I remember my parents were in town visiting the day that Bruce was caught cheating on a science test. As a parent, I was upset at hearing the news, and expected Walt to really give his grandson the gears. But he just laughed and said, "It's not cheating if you don't get caught." I thought, *Jesus, that's all he needs right now, more encouragement.*

Bruce's ability to freestyle rap at a moment's notice made him even more popular among his classmates, one of which was a kid named Jacob, who quickly became one of Bruce's best friends. They had sleepovers together all the time, either at our place or at Jacob's, and he even came up to our cottage with us a couple of times. Jacob was a decent kid, and he seemed like a good match for Bruce at the time. They both loved rap music, and they both played basketball.

Bruce and Jacob were up for anything, so long as they got to do it together—which eventually included marijuana. It wasn't that Jacob was a bad influence on Bruce. If anything, they became bad influences on each other, each egging the other one on into taking bigger and bigger risks.

At Linden Christian, Bruce also met the girl who became his first girlfriend, and they went on to date for a number of years. Unfortunately, I'm not sure her family ever thought Bruce was a great match for their daughter, and on some level I understood why. Here was this kid who boxed and was obsessed with rap music—from the outside, he could appear to be a bit of a bad boy. It was only once you got to know him that you realized it was mostly an act. After all, how much of a rebel could you really be if you brought your old baby blanket to every boxing match?

Mostly, but not entirely. Bruce did get himself into real trouble a couple of times. I chalk this up in part to that criminal lifestyle he admired so much, and in part to his natural proclivity for taking chances and pushing the limit.

Once I remember seeing a letter in our mailbox addressed to

Bruce from a local restorative justice program. I opened it and learned that he'd been caught shoplifting a DVD from Zellers. Of course, he hadn't told us about it. I called the program's offices, and learned they'd also tried contacting Bruce by phone several times, which he'd also brushed off. I guess he figured that if he ignored the whole situation, it would just go away. That evening, I confronted Bruce about it, then dragged him to see a lawyer I know, who told him, "Look, you need to tell me exactly what happened—no bullshit." He came clean about the theft, and ended up attending the restorative justice sessions so that the whole incident could be put to bed.

The good news, at least, was that some of Bruce's more extreme behaviours seemed to have stabilized by the time he got to high school. The physical tics he struggled with when he was younger had disappeared on their own, although Anne and I did sometimes wonder whether Bruce had simply found new ways of disguising them from us. He'd also been prescribed Ritalin after leaving the Tourette's clinic, and it seemed to help. He would take a pill each morning and from there was better able to buckle down and pay attention at school. By the time Bruce got home, the effects had largely worn off, but to Anne and me that was secondary. The only thing we cared about was getting through the school day.

Bruce wasn't really opposed to taking Ritalin, but we did have to remind him all the time to take it. Plus, he had a good friend at school named Ken, who was also on the same medication, and together they came up with a ritual they called called Rit-Free Fridays, where they'd both go off their meds for the day. This made the two of them more disruptive than usual, although I also think it made them feel a little more natural, and more like themselves. Rit-Free Fridays led to more conflict at school, but on some level I understood the impulse. After all, how many people who are on medication start to suspect they don't actually need their meds after all, and wonder what they'd be like without them?

The best advocate for medicine in our house was Anne, in large part because, when Bruce was in high school, she went back to school herself to get her nursing degree. Her mother and her aunt had passed away in short succession, and Anne had taken care of both of them in their final days. She soon realized that nursing was her true calling. Her initial plan was to take the courses at her own pace, but she really fell in love with it, and ended up graduating on the Dean's List in the standard timeline. She got a job with the regional health authority as a palliative care nurse, and would visit the homes of people who had months—sometimes even weeks—to live, administering their medication and making sure they were comfortable. She only worked part-time, but she absolutely loved it.

I used to joke that part of the reason Anne went back to school was because she got tired of waiting for me to come home. Starting in the mid-'90s, I'd moved on from local sports and the CFL into a full-time role with *Hockey Night in Canada*—which meant I was on the road as much as ever. I felt pretty healthy, all things considered, but Anne used to tell me stories about patients she'd worked with who were my age, and then suddenly I wouldn't feel so well for the next couple of hours.

Back in Winnipeg, Bruce was developing a love of sports of his own. For grades 10 to 12, he attended Tuxedo-Shaftesbury High School, where he made the varsity basketball team. Like boxing, this was another sport he was interested in, and he shot a lot of hoops around the neighbourhood even outside of school. Late in his grade 12 year, Bruce had entered a three-on-three basketball tournament with his friends Jacob and Ken. But Ken got injured in a car accident at the last minute and couldn't play. So instead, Bruce recruited one of his neighbours to replace him: an athletic phenom named Ryan Reaves. (Now a noted tough guy for the Toronto Maple Leafs, Ryan was also an incredibly talented basketball and football player, and he grew up good buddies with both Bruce and Darcy. Whenever I'd get home from work and see a pair of size-15 sneakers sitting in our front hallway, I knew Ryan was over.)

Academically, though, there were ongoing issues. Anne and I went to parent-teacher interviews together, and every year we gritted our teeth and expected the worst. It was his grade 12 English teacher, Mrs. Smith, however, who caught us the most by surprise. She told us, "Bruce is a really talented writer, but I just don't know what I'm going to get from him day to day." We knew that was a reflection of his ADHD and everything that was underpinning it. But we drove home that night feeling encouraged that at least someone saw potential in him.

"That's pretty good, isn't it?" I said to Anne, beaming.

It didn't help that by the end of grade 12, Bruce had pretty much stopped taking his medication altogether. But try as we might, we couldn't force Bruce to take it. Ultimately, it was his decision, and when Anne and I talked about it, we decided that once graduation came, he would have to start living with the consequences.

Although even graduation didn't come without a moment of shock. When Anne and I arrived at the ceremony for Bruce's graduating class, we got a copy of the program and immediately flipped to the Os—and Bruce's name wasn't on it.

"This can't be real," I said to Anne. "Is this Bruce's biggest scam of all time? Did he actually trick us into thinking he finished high school?"

After some brief panic, we were able to confirm that it was just an error in the program. Bruce really had graduated. And soon enough, he did march across that stage, to the cheers of his parents and classmates alike.

With Ritalin a thing of the past, Bruce's oppositional behaviour became impossible to ignore. Each day in our house became a battleground, where Bruce would argue with seemingly every single rule and decision Anne and I made, from chores to curfew. If there was something to argue about, Bruce would find a way to disagree with us. This was difficult for the three of us, and Darcy often got roped into it, too. He witnessed more of Bruce's risk-taking behaviour than Anne or I did, and he was torn between ratting on him and being loyal to his big brother. I remember one Christmas in Amherst, when Bruce and his cousin packed Darcy in the backseat of their grandfather's car and went looking for weed. When they got back, Darcy was horror-stricken and came to me right away to tell me where they'd been. I was furious with Bruce, but oddly Bruce never held it against Darcy.

At the time, however, Bruce couldn't see any of these warning signs. Despite the challenges, he had become a popular kid, with close friends, a girlfriend, and, eventually, a car.

Like a lot of kids, Bruce had been advocating for his driver's license long before he turned sixteen. When the fateful birthday finally came, Anne signed him for lessons. But he didn't seem to absorb any of the information, and ended up failing the road test four times in a

row. I remember taking Bruce over for one such attempt, only for him to come back through the door thirty seconds later.

"Aren't you taking the test?" I asked him.

"It's over," Bruce said glumly.

It turned out he'd gone straight through the stop sign at the end of the parking lot and his instructor had failed him on the spot.

Finally, Bruce passed the test on his fifth attempt, and then the battle shifted to whether he could have access to one of the family vehicles. In fact, the very same day he got his driver's license, Bruce casually asked me if he could borrow my Dodge Ram pickup for the night. I told him no. I didn't think he was ready yet.

"Ready? What do you mean? I passed my test!"

This quickly became another well-worn argument. Bruce wanted to borrow the truck whenever I was out of town, which, of course, was pretty much every weekend. The conversation always followed the same structure: I'd say no, he'd wear me down, and I'd let him, just to stop the arguing.

As a way of resolving that particular argument, we eventually bought him his own car. It was a beater that was barely on this side of being a write-off, and it didn't take long for Bruce to push it over the line, as he managed to wrap it around a telephone pole on the way home from school one day. He swore it only happened because he had to swerve to avoid hitting a cat, but I know it was really because he was driving too fast and lost control of the vehicle. There were a couple of his friends in the car with him, and it's a miracle that nobody ended up getting hurt.

Even when he was driving someone else's vehicle, Bruce wasn't much more careful. One time while up at the cottage, he and his girlfriend took my truck down to nearby Falcon Lake for a party. When they got back to the cottage, Bruce told me that someone had hit the truck while it was parked. I went out to inspect it, and in the darkness I could see a bit of damage to the right front fender. When we got back to Winnipeg, Bruce and I took the truck in to have it looked at by an insurance investigator, and she took one look at the broken fender before pulling a piece of tree bark out of the opening.

"Nobody hit you," she said, looking at Bruce. "You ran into a tree."

She told us as clearly as possible how serious insurance fraud is, and told us that if we withdrew the claim, she would forget about the whole thing. I was relieved to be let off the hook so easily, and furious with Bruce about lying about what had happened to the truck. But as soon as she left the room, Bruce turned to me, totally unfazed, and said, "Let's go to another place and see what they say."

Once he had regular access to a car, Bruce could've been anywhere. That freedom, of course, is a dream for many teenagers, but for Bruce it also led him into some less-than-ideal situations—especially once he started smoking weed regularly.

One night, Bruce told us he was going to a movie, but Anne was pretty sure that was a lie. So she decided to go full *Starsky & Hutch*, with Darcy by her side. They got into the van and drove over to the local Mac's—where, sure enough, she saw Bruce out front buying weed. But she was smart enough to not confront him about it outright. Instead, she called him on his cell phone and asked what he was doing.

"Oh, I'm just going into the movie," he said.

"That's funny," Anne replied, "because I'm outside the Mac's right now and I can see you buying weed."

The weed thing bothered Anne and me so much because we were both concerned it might lead to something more serious. Whenever we would argue with Bruce, it always came back to these poor choices he was making, because we all knew he had a tendency to push things even further than the average teenager. Privately, I also worried that Bruce might have inherited some less-than-pleasant genes from my side of the family. There is a history of binge drinking on my father's side, and the last thing I wanted was for Bruce to be susceptible to similar problems.

Anne and I were never sure whether Bruce was doing any other drugs while in high school. Then again, we weren't educated in the ways of drug use, or warning signs to look out for. Not yet.

"I'm Not a Junkie"

Bruce graduated from Shaftesbury in June 2003. But it wasn't clear to anyone—least of all Bruce himself—what he was going to do with the rest of his life. We knew he wasn't going to go to post-secondary, since high school had been enough of an academic challenge for him. And after losing at the Canada Games, his fascination with boxing was fading.

A few months before graduation, Bruce went off to Montreal to train for three weeks under a buddy of mine named Russ Anber, who I'd done commentary with at the Olympics. It was a helpful experience—even though Bruce never put in the required roadwork, despite Russ's insistence—and he came back a better boxer for it.

That fall, he signed up to fight at a show in Winnipeg against a guy named Kent Brown, who was a member of the national team and who'd fought in the Commonwealth Games. The fight was part of the buildup for Olympic Trials that were going to be held in Regina the following year. Bruce fought hard, but he was no match for Brown's strength and veteran savvy. That defeat seemed to take much of the remaining wind out of his sails. Bruce fought one more time, for the provincial championship, but this time he wasn't as committed to his training in the lead-up. Without fitness on his side, Bruce knew he had to win in the first round, or he was going to run out of gas. It was the latter outcome. This other kid wasn't as talented as Bruce, but he was in better shape, and in boxing that's often what it comes down to.

It was a dispiriting loss, and after that Bruce never fought again.

With both high school and his fledgling boxing career behind him, Bruce suddenly found himself with a bunch of free time on his hands.

He worked for a summer with the Green Team, a government-funded program that gave students experience working in nature, near our cottage. He made a couple of friends among his coworkers, but other than that I don't think he impressed a lot of people over there. To be frank, Bruce hated the job—he was an urban kid at heart—and I later heard from a couple of people involved that they would have fired him if they could. After that first summer was over, he didn't come back the next year.

Privately, Anne and I hoped that now was the time he would go out and find a steady job, and start becoming a responsible adult, and we had a plan to motivate him. Bruce was still antsy about having his own vehicle, and he used to borrow my truck to get to and from his shifts with the Green Team. Anne and I agreed to buy him, at his request, a Chevrolet Blazer—with the idea that we would make the first three payments, and after that Bruce had to take care of them himself.

It worked out to something like $350 or $400 per month, which we felt was a reasonable target to shoot for. The challenge was in finding a solid job that would generate the money in the first place.

Anne and I were on him all the time to go out and look for work. Bruce was still living at home, and when I got home from my own workday, I used to go downstairs to the basement and say to him, "Bruce, did anyone come down here today and offer you a job?" This sarcastic approach didn't seem to motivate him much, but then again nothing else did, either. At various points we used to threaten charging Bruce rent if he wasn't going to even try, but I think he knew we weren't serious and nothing ever came of it.

Somehow, Bruce did end up getting a job working at a local call centre. Not just that, but he managed to stick with it long enough to actually make a few payments on the Blazer. It wasn't the most glamorous job in the world, but Anne and I were relieved that he'd found something to occupy him for eight hours each day. Things seemed to be going pretty well, even as Bruce's driving abilities continued to pose problems. The Blazer was a standard, which he didn't actually know how to drive, and he was constantly damn near blowing the clutch out of it.

Unfortunately, Bruce's taste for petty crime soon resurfaced, and even started to escalate.

I don't want to make him sound like he was constantly breaking the law, but when he did, let's just say it wasn't well thought out. In high school, for instance, he had a fake ID he'd bought off a classmate, and he used it to get into bars and nightclubs. No big deal.

But not long afterwards, he had his actual license suspended over a couple of speeding tickets, and when he went to get it reinstated at the motor vehicle department, he handed over the fake one as proof of his real identity. Unfortunately, this building also happened to be the headquarters for the Manitoba RCMP, so when the person behind the counter took one look at the fake ID, they called over the Mounties, who in turn called the Winnipeg police.

Bruce showed that same attention to detail in his brief stint as a counterfeiter. It all started one day when Anne found a stack of linen paper in Bruce's bedroom in the basement. She didn't know what it was, let alone what it was used for, but it seemed strange. We asked Bruce about it, and he told us some innocuous-sounding story that we couldn't prove or disprove, so we dropped it. A few weeks later, Bruce was fired from his job at the call centre, and blamed it on cutbacks across the company.

We weren't able to connect the dots on those two incidents until years later, when one of the friends involved came clean to me about what really happened: Bruce, along with a couple of friends, were making and distributing fake paper bills. Hence the stash of linen paper. I can't speak to their level of craftsmanship, but there were enough of these bills made and distributed (or attempted to be distributed) that the police got involved. In fact, I was told, the real reason Bruce was fired from the call centre is that the cops showed up to the building while he was on shift and hauled him out of there in handcuffs, in front of everyone. The only reason Bruce managed to keep it a secret from Anne and me is that he was assigned a lawyer through Legal Aid, who was able to get the case thrown out due to an illegal search. (Darcy, I found out later, had heard about it through his own social circle.)

Had we known about the counterfeiting at the time, I'm honestly not sure what Anne and I would have done about it. Confiscate the no-longer-harmless-looking linen paper? Call the police and turn him in ourselves? Thinking back on it now, this was the beginning of Bruce getting in over his head, and his impulsive, risk-taking behaviour putting him in some serious danger.

For most people, this incident would be a sign to stop screwing around and get on the straight and narrow. But not for Bruce.

And Anne and I were just trying to survive each new problem as it came up—we only realized in retrospect that Bruce was heading out of the frying pan and into the fire.

One morning we were up at the cottage in Whiteshell Provincial Park and we got a call from Bruce.

"The police were here last night," he said cheerfully.

"What?" I said, my heart rate spiking. "Why?"

It turned out that the previous evening he'd gone through the drive-thru at our local Wendy's, where he knew the guy who was working the window. As a joke, Bruce pulled out a BB gun he had with him and showed it to the guy when he pulled around to get his food. They were kidding around, but someone else called the cops, and they showed up at our house to figure out what was going on. They brought Bruce into the squad car and explained the seriousness of the situation, but ended up letting him go without charges. Bruce was anxious to call Anne and me because he wanted to break the news to us before the cops could.

"You've got to be fucking kidding me," I said. Anne took the phone from me and gave it to Bruce a second time. We were furious.

Then, not to be outdone, Darcy grabbed the phone for his turn to rub it in.

"Nice work, Bruce," he said.

I ended up speaking to the police officer on the phone as well. He confirmed that, in this case, Bruce had actually come clean and told us the entire truth. And he reminded me how serious this incident was. I think he could tell we were concerned parents, doing their best, but he said that Bruce needed to straighten himself out, and fast.

While this was all going on, it became obvious to us that Bruce was smoking weed—mostly because he wasn't particularly subtle about hiding it. He once hotboxed his mother's van, for instance, unconcerned with how long the smell would linger for afterwards. Another time I was reaching down into the handle of my truck, and came across a dime bag he'd forgotten to take with him. And once I went down to the basement, where I discovered the window wide open and Bruce and Darcy sitting underneath it, smoking a joint together. (In that last situation, at least, Bruce willingly took all of the blame as the older brother.)

This wasn't a huge cause for concern on its own. Plenty of teenagers smoked weed, after all, and turned out just fine. Anne and I just hoped it wouldn't lead to anything else.

We tried talking to Bruce about the dangers of doing drugs multiple times. I also told him there had been problems in my family, mostly to do with alcohol, and that for that reason he had to be extra careful. But it was in one ear and out the other. Like any teenager, Bruce probably thought, *Whatever. I'm young, I'll live forever, that can't happen to me.*

•   •   •

During that first year after Bruce graduated, just the sound of the phone ringing would make my heart race.

It was a chaotic time. Bruce had little structure in his life, and no interest in any kind of honest, conventional nine-to-five job. His oppositional behaviour was as strong as ever, and the constant arguing wore us all out. Meanwhile, Anne and I continued to worry that his drug use would escalate into something more serious, especially considering what else he seemed to be doing in his free time. One day, for instance, he came home with a set of tires and shiny chrome rims for his Blazer. I asked him how he'd gotten them, since he obviously didn't have enough money to buy them himself. He came up with some nonsense about someone owing him money and giving him the tires as payment. Another time he walked in the door with a laptop, and claimed that he got it from another friend. To me, this set off alarm bells that Bruce had started dealing drugs—how else was he affording this stuff? I told him to give the laptop back immediately. To Bruce's credit, he did, albeit reluctantly.

The other lingering factor in our minds was that Bruce was an adult now. He was old enough to be on the front lines of Afghanistan, for crying out loud. So how involved should we really be? At a certain point, he was going to need to take responsibility for his own life.

Things came to a head one day when Darcy noticed something unusual in the ceiling of Bruce's bedroom, and when he looked more closely, he found a vial of steroids and a needle. Darcy reluctantly showed this to Anne, and another heated argument ensued. Bruce, once again, made up some complicated lie, this time about how the steroids weren't his, and how he wasn't the one using them. Even when confronted with the evidence, Bruce wasn't strategic enough to repent, get rid of the vials, and promise not to do it again.

The arguing was one thing. But equally taxing to Anne and me was how good Bruce had become at lying. It was scary how effortlessly these wildly false statements would fly out of his mouth. It got to the point where I would just assume he was lying before he'd even finished his sentence—and most of the time I'd be right.

Shortly after the steroids incident, Bruce and Darcy got into an argument in the living room, which quickly escalated into a full-on wrestling match. They crashed around the floor trying to get at one another, and eventually Bruce broke a leg off of my favourite recliner.

It was all too much, and finally I'd had enough. I told Bruce, "I'm going to the lumberyard to get a piece of wood to fix that chair. And when I get back, you better not be here." Sure enough, when I got back home, he'd packed his bags and taken off.

Officially getting kicked out of the house happened in the heat of the moment, but it came as no surprise to anyone living under our roof. Anne and I had warned Bruce multiple times about illegal drugs, and the risks of leading such a reckless lifestyle. The only real surprise—to Bruce, as well as to Anne and me—was that this time we'd actually followed through on doing something about it. Finding that syringe and those vials in our home was a breaking point, and something had to change in a big way.

The fact that it was steroids in particular bothered me. If it was something like ecstasy or more weed, I think our first impulse would've been to help, in some way. But as far as I was concerned, steroids were purely for vanity. Even though he was done with boxing, Bruce had decided that part of the gangster lifestyle was being jacked. So I guessed this was his way of filling out and getting more muscular. But he was doing it all wrong. Rather than training the old-fashioned way, Bruce was looking for a magic shortcut. He didn't realize that steroids don't do anything on their own. You still have to do the work.

The next morning, Bruce called. I answered right away.

"I hate you guys," he said. "Because of you, I'm living in my car."

He was trying to tug at my heartstrings, but this time I stood my ground. "Well," I said, "I guess you'll figure it out."

Sure enough, he ended up at his girlfriend's house, where her parents had reluctantly agreed he could stay for the next couple of weeks. During that time we didn't have a lot of contact with him. I did meet with his girlfriend's father once for coffee, and we discussed the logistics of Bruce living there and what Anne and I could do to reduce the burden. He told me he was keeping Bruce occupied by having him take apart an old deck at their house, which seemed like a good idea. But other than that, Anne and I didn't really know what he was doing. We just hoped he'd take the right lessons from the situation.

Eventually Bruce did come back home, and we tried to make things work. He walked in the front door that first day a little sheepish, maybe, but nowhere near repentant. Anne and I were happy to have our son back beneath our roof, but we were also nervous. Had we made the right decision in sending him away? Would anything change, or would he just revert to his old habits?

Right away, it became clear that Bruce's time away had mostly given him a taste for independence, and it wasn't long before he decided to move back out again, this time for good. He and a buddy moved into a house together in St. Boniface, down the street from the hospital there.

It was stressful to have Bruce out of our sight once again, and especially so quickly after the first ill-fated attempt. At first, though, there were signs that Bruce might actually be turning things around. After moving out of our house, he managed to get a job helping an acquaintance of his hang sheets of drywall. But it was too good to be true. After just a couple of days, Bruce was fired because he was caught doing drugs—he never told me which ones—while at work.

Now, when Bruce came home to visit, he didn't look good. He'd lost a lot of weight and was generally run-down. Anne and I told him that if there was a problem with drugs, he just had to tell us, and we would help him. But as usual, he denied everything. We never gave him a drug test or anything, so we never knew conclusively, but it was becoming obvious just to look at him that he was in trouble.

In between his visits, Anne and I both started doing some basic research with Dr. Google, looking up the basic signs of drug addiction and what to do about them. Bruce's physical changes all seemed to fit the bill. The other thing I learned was that most drug users follow the same path of consumption. They started by taking the drugs orally. When that doesn't work fast enough, they started grinding them up and snorting them. And when they need it even faster than that, they melted the drugs down and injected them directly into their blood.

How far down that path, I wondered, was Bruce now?

Unfortunately, we were about to find out. Bruce wasn't entirely happy with the house he'd moved into, and so he and his friend

Jacob found a different place in the core area of Winnipeg. From the moment they first moved in, Anne and I grew more and more concerned about Bruce's drug use and how the two friends might be enabling one another. But even we didn't realize how fully Bruce had descended into the gangster lifestyle that he'd idolized for so many years.

It all came to a boil one weekend in February 2007, when I was in Calgary getting ready to host a game for *Hockey Night in Canada*. I was actually in a cab headed to the rink on Saturday when Darcy called me and told me there was a problem. "Something's going on with Bruce," he said. "I think he got beat up."

My heart jumped right back to my throat. I called Bruce right away and when he picked up, I could hear the fear in his voice.

"What's going on, Bruce?"

He started telling me about a friend of his from high school, who had become a member of a local street gang and was now dealing drugs. Somewhere along the way, this guy decided he was going to use Bruce and Jacob's house as a stash house. Meanwhile, Bruce had also started "making drops"—delivering drugs, in other words—for this guy. It was a messy business to be caught up in. Then, Bruce said, yesterday the guy showed up at the house and accused him of breaking into the stash for his personal use.

"He told me, 'You owe me $25,000,'" Bruce said on the phone. "Which is obviously bullshit, Dad."

That afternoon, however, the gang member came back to the house—this time with an enforcer. The enforcer was holding a club, and he was there to punish Bruce for not paying the money back. When the first shot came down, Bruce told me he held up one hand

74

to protect his head, and the bones shattered on impact. I shudder to think what might have happened to his skull, had the club hit its intended target. It must've been a horrifying scene.

In lieu of the cash he supposedly owed them, the two men made Bruce sign over the ownership of his Blazer to them. Then they made him write out a note affirming that he was giving the vehicle away of his own free will. This struck me, even then, as the work of a less-than-criminal-mastermind, and my thoughts were already racing, wondering how any court of law could take such a document seriously. (I later saw a copy of the note and felt confirmed in my snap judgement—it was literally written in crayon.)

There was more to Bruce's story. Their new vehicle now acquired, the gang member and his enforcer told Bruce they might have to come back for more later. Then they ripped the gold chain off his neck and left.

"I gotta get out of Winnipeg," he said in conclusion.

I agreed, but told him not to do anything yet, and promised to look into it right away.

I hung up the phone, my heart in my throat, and took a deep breath to calm my mind.

The broadcast was in a couple of hours. I couldn't up and leave, but I couldn't focus on anything but Bruce's situation. I tried making a few other calls, but the Saddledome is notoriously bad for cell phone service. You've got to be in certain areas in order to get any reception at all. The only place I could find that got a decent signal was down on one of the benches at ice level, which is where my calls to a lawyer we knew in Winnipeg finally connected. Unfortunately, he didn't answer, and I was soon out of time.

I called Bruce back and asked if he had a safe place to stay that night. He said yes—so I did the game, somehow.

I have no idea how I got through it, and I'm pretty sure my colleague, Kelly Hrudey, sensed something was wrong. We managed to do the game itself, as well as the half-hour postgame show, which felt painful and endless. But my trip still wasn't over: that night I was scheduled to take a redeye flight to Toronto and then on to Moncton for my mother's seventy-fifth birthday. Again, I felt I had no choice.

When the plane landed early the next morning, my brother Stuart picked me up from the airport, and in the entire forty-five-minute drive to our parents' house in Amherst, I didn't say a word about what had happened to Bruce. Internally, I was worried sick.

But Bruce had been in trouble before, and we'd always made it through, so on some level I told myself this was just more of the same. Instead, I became fixated on wanting to get through the weekend and not spoil the festivities for everyone else—and that included Anne. She had already left for the East Coast when the assault happened, and when we saw each other that first night in Amherst, I didn't even tell her.

My poker face didn't last long. By Monday morning, Anne could tell I was hiding something. I cracked, and told her what I knew about the situation, and she dialled Bruce's number immediately to hear it in his own words. She wasn't angry with me, just shocked at what had happened. It was me who was angry—at myself, for trying to contain the situation and carry on as if everything was okay, rather than just being honest. I should have told Anne right away, just like I should never have gone through with the broadcast in the first place.

While I was berating myself, Anne got Bruce on the phone. He admitted to her that he was in serious trouble this time, and then he said something that made both of our hearts sink: "I'm not a junkie, Mom. I just use occasionally."

This was as close to a full-fledged confession as we'd ever gotten from him before. In that moment everything changed, and we finally understood just how bad Bruce's problems had become. But first we had to deal with the threat, which was not just against Bruce, but our entire family.

These guys knew Bruce didn't have $25,000. The real message they were sending was: *Get it from your family.* It's an old strategy and an effective one, because there are plenty of families out there who would find a way to come up with that amount of money if it meant getting their kid out of danger. But with gangs, the police later told us, a debt like that never truly goes away. Once they sense weakness, they'll come back for more, and before you know it, they'll have your house, your car—everything you own.

We knew we had to do something, but Anne and I were still thousands of kilometres away and the next available flight wasn't until the following day. We had no choice but to stick to our original plans. In the meantime, we put Bruce up in a hotel far away from the scene of the crime, and sent Darcy to stay with him. We also got a family friend to check in on them and make sure things were okay. Both brothers were understandably still frightened, but I think that closeness must have been good for them—at the very least, they managed to ring up a honking huge room service bill together.

Okay, I thought, *that's settled. What next?*

We happened to have another lawyer friend who worked with the Winnipeg police, so, not knowing what else to do, I called him and told him what had happened. He said to leave it with him and someone would get back to us shortly. Sure enough, within the hour, we got a call from the head of the gang unit. He was already familiar with the guy who had orchestrated the assault on Bruce. He asked me, "Where is your son now? I'm going to put a detail together and go put him into protective custody."

When I heard that, my brain went into panic mode. *Whoa, wait a minute!* The situation seemed to be spiralling out of control. Everything was happening so quickly. Anne and I were prepared to put our faith in the police, but I still wanted to have some say over the situation—or at least feel like I did. So I asked if we could at least wait until Anne and I got back home, and then I would bring Bruce in myself. The officer agreed.

The next morning, we flew back on the first available flight, and met Darcy and Bruce back at our house.

I took one look at Bruce and knew right away that the story he'd told Anne about his drug use wasn't true. He looked sickly and pale. He was thinner than ever, with darker circles under his eyes than ever before. Even discounting the broken hand that was now wrapped in bandages, this was not a person who used "occasionally." Bruce was clearly addicted. And he needed help before he was in any condition to go to the police.

So we got right back in the car and took Bruce to the Health Sciences Centre, which is the major hospital in Winnipeg. We got there around 8 or 9 p.m., and waited for several hours for Bruce to be seen by a doctor. It was another painful experience, because whatever drug Bruce had been on—meth, or maybe oxy, I still wasn't sure—he was now coming down, and it wasn't pretty. I sat in that waiting room with my twenty-year-old son in my lap, trying to calm him down and hold on to him. His brain had shifted into panic mode, and he was desperate to leave. It took everything I had to only barely convince him to stay.

When we finally got into a room, it took the doctor all of ten seconds to identify the problem: substance abuse. He told us we had two choices for treatment. The first was sending Bruce to Addictions Foundation of Manitoba, or AFM. This was a free, government-run centre, but as such had a waitlist of four to six weeks. The second option was shelling out for a private centre, where Bruce could be seen right away.

Anne and I knew immediately we wanted to go the private route. Sure, it would be expensive. But in that moment, time was everything. We were willing to pay whatever it took to find an immediate solution.

First, though, Bruce could get into a short-term detox program run by the hospital. It would take a couple of days for a bed to open up, and in the meantime the doctor wrote Bruce a small prescription for Oxycontin, then he was sent home.

The next morning, we had an appointment with the detox doctor. Her name was Lindy Lee, and she was a lovely woman who had devoted her life to helping those suffering from substance abuse. She told us she would have a bed ready for Bruce within four days.

Those next few days were a challenge for Bruce. Luckily, he had a top-notch nurse there by his side. Anne was compassionate, knowledgeable, and experienced—and she was Bruce's mother. In short, the perfect person to look after him while he recovered at home with us. She made sure to dole out the prescribed pills on schedule, and Bruce spent most of his time in his room—upstairs, this time, and not in the basement—calm and sedate. But he was clearly used to being able to take it whenever he wanted, and sticking to the doctor's prescribed schedule was hard on him. At one point he actually stole an extra pill when Anne wasn't looking, just to fend off the impending dope sickness.

Meanwhile, I was still worried about our family's safety. I had taken Bruce down to the police station, as I'd promised I would, and he had made an official statement about the assault. Again, we were relieved to see the police were taking this seriously. We hadn't even left the building by the time they'd obtained warrants and were getting ready to grab everyone they could who was associated with the assault.

But what if the gang figured out Bruce was home again and decided to make good on its threat? It was terrifying. Luckily, the Police Service agreed to assign two cops to stay in our house, around the clock, until Bruce could get into detox. That made me feel better—in part because the cops were all hockey fans, so we passed the time by watching games together and shooting the breeze.

For Anne, however, the new arrangement was a bit traumatic. To her, having these cops suddenly everywhere was an invasion of privacy, and the house didn't feel like our home anymore. I understood how she felt, and did my best to remind her that this was temporary, and that we would get through it together. While this was all going on she was also back in school yet again, this time taking her master's degree to become a nurse practitioner. She'd only just started the program when the assault happened. The aftermath took up so much of our time and energy that at one point she had to call one of her professors and explain why she couldn't give an assigned presentation on time. (The professor readily agreed, and then quipped: "That is the best dog-ate-my-homework story I've ever heard.")

The morning of detox arrived. Bruce got himself ready to go, and I remember the cops getting in their cars and waving at us as they drove away. Just in case, they gave Anne and me a pair of handheld alarms, where you could summon a cop car to your location with the push of a button. We kept those on us for two or three weeks afterwards, but thankfully never had to use them.

Bruce was in detox at Health Sciences for about a week. He never argued with us about going, especially after meeting with Dr. Lee, and on the whole it felt like a more collaborative process. His main concern was that he wouldn't be able to see his girlfriend as easily. But other than that, he adapted to it quite well. Sometimes when we called the communal phone, he would answer it himself: "Detox ward, Bruce speaking!"

After dropping him off, I breathed a sigh of relief. Now we were finally on the right track. The night we'd brought him home from Health Sciences, I went straight to the computer to find Bruce the right private facility. I googled "treatment centres," and the first result that came up was for a fancy-looking place with a 1-800 number to call. Honest to God, I assumed it was in Winnipeg. It took me about three phone calls with their staff to figure out they were all the way in Toronto. But by that point they'd already done an intake interview with Bruce from his detox bed, to see if he was an acceptable candidate for treatment, and the wheels were in motion. The program cost $20,000 for six weeks.

At our initial meeting, Dr. Lee had told us that Bruce had issues with more than one drug, which matched something he had casually told us years earlier: "You know nobody under forty *just* drinks, right?" When you're deeply into that lifestyle, it's not just one thing—it's everything.

When his stint at Health Sciences was up, I drove Bruce straight from detox to the airport, and the two of us flew off to Toronto. That might sound sudden, but it's actually the preferred way of doing things. Anne and I were still learning as we went, but we'd been told that you should never give an addict the option of going home for a few days and getting their life together. That's just an invitation to start using again. And this time, Bruce didn't fight us. He knew it was the only way.

It was a whirlwind couple of weeks, but once Bruce had been accepted to the private treatment centre, Anne and I finally had a chance to catch our breath. A lot of our decision-making to that point had been almost businesslike: we dealt with one issue, and then the next one, and then the next one. But when Bruce was accepted to the centre in Toronto, we both heaved a huge sigh of relief. It was as if a massive weight had been removed from both of our shoulders.

"This is where he needs to be," I said to Anne that evening. "This is going to work."

Despite our mistakes along the way, we were proud that we hadn't given up on Bruce. No matter how fraught things had become, we'd never lost contact. Even though every late-night phone call made my heart jump up past my throat, I was glad that he was still making the call in the first place. Plus, Anne and I were extremely fortunate in that we were always on the same page. We never pointed fingers at each other or second-guessed the other person's ideas. We were in accord on every decision we ever made for Bruce—and every decision came from a place of love.

In that interim period Anne and I also had time to reflect on the nature of addiction, and how it can resurface in families across generations. She used to remind me, "All I know is it doesn't come from my family!" And that was true. Anne came from a farming family just outside of Brandon, and drugs and alcohol weren't a factor on either side of her family tree. Whereas I knew the addictive gene was very much present in my family. So it made sense it would show up in our children's lives, too. It would have been nice if the gene had skipped a generation, but it didn't.

The other thing we used to remind each other of was that no matter how difficult the situation seemed for us, it was always much harder for Bruce. There was certainly anger and frustration in our relationship with him in those years, but underpinning those emotions was always love. Darcy used to quote a line from the comedian Mitch Hedberg, about how addiction is the only disease you can get yelled at for having. Imagine standing over a cancer patient and shouting, "What are you doing with all that cancer? Get rid of it!" The more we all learned about how addiction works, the more we realized what a heavy toll it must have been taking on Bruce's mind, as well as his body.

Five

Airlift to Toronto

If you'd have been there when Bruce and I flew from Winnipeg to Toronto, you might've assumed it was a prisoner evacuation rather than a trip to an addiction treatment centre. With the gang threat still hanging above our heads, the police ended up accompanying us to the airport. Once we got there, they shepherded us into a special private security line—which moves a lot faster than the normal one—and then onto the plane. Finally, we took our seats and the airlift was complete.

Bruce was doing his best to appear calm, but I wondered whether he was secretly nervous about what was in store for him. Anne and I had spent days trying to sell him on the idea of a private treatment centre, and how it would be good for him. We showed him the facility website, and it looked like a lovely place. I remember Bruce reading through their list of amenities and finally coming around when he saw they offered massages. That made me laugh. I thought to myself, *Do you have any idea where you're going, or what you're going for?* Looking back on it, that was probably one of the first warning signs that he was doing this more for us than for himself.

When the flight landed, we took a cab to the treatment centre, and now Bruce's nerves came to the surface. He was noticeably jittery and not saying much. We went inside the centre together, where we met the staff and got a brief tour. I have to say, I was impressed. I didn't have any other experience with treatment centres to compare it to, but to me it appeared to be a high-end, professionally run operation. The orientation process was smooth and professional, too. Bruce seemed like he was in good hands.

During the tour, we got to see the common areas, the fitness centre, and the on-site clinic. They didn't take us inside any group sessions or anything, which I understood, because we were obviously outsiders and needed to respect their space. We also saw where Bruce's bedroom would be. In recovery, I learned, it's typical to have two people per room, and this one looked comfortable and clean— like a nice hotel room.

Looking around, I kept thinking, *He's in the right place now. He'll do well here.*

Bruce, on the other hand, had become visibly anxious from the moment we walked through the front doors. For him, this was the unknown. For the next six weeks, he was going to have to give up control of his life, and he wouldn't have any of his friends, family, or routines to fall back on while he did it. It was going to be a big shock to his system.

I have to admit, there was something darkly comic about Bruce's sudden onset of nerves. After all, this was the guy who'd spent years declaring how tough and dangerous he was—and the thing that ended up scaring him more than anything was a comfortable room in a comfortable building where all of his needs would be taken care of. But that's the power of addiction. Oxycontin is a horribly addictive drug, and coming off it is really, really hard.

Thanks to his stint in detox at Health Sciences, when Bruce arrived at the centre, he was clean and, in theory, should have been able to get by without any other drugs in his system while living there. But that's a lot easier said than done. Drug addicts experience intense cravings that can last for months. It's been said that it takes a full year to get the receptors in your brain to fire properly again. In the meantime, every day—every hour—can be a struggle. On top of those physiological changes, there's the massive change in routine. As I came to understand later, addicts use drugs to deal with anything that happens in their lives. And here was Bruce, suddenly going to a place where he knows he's about to lose his entire way of coping with life. That would be a scary thing for anyone to reckon with.

When the tour was over, Bruce and I said our goodbyes.

"Remember, Bruce, you're going to do well here," I said to him. "You can change your life. Just do the work and you'll be okay."

He looked nervous, but nodded. "Thanks, Dad."

I told him I would call him, and reminded him that he could call home anytime he needed to.

Then I got into another cab and left, thinking only one thing: *Christ, what a relief.*

Back in Winnipeg, Anne and I both were just so relieved that

Bruce was in a safe place, and that he was getting the help that he needed. It wasn't on our shoulders anymore; now it was in the hands of professionals. We felt like we'd done the best we could. We hadn't just sat back and waited for him to clear the waitlist for AFM. Instead, we were being proactive, and shelling out for a high-end private facility that came strongly recommended. How could this not work? And when it did, we figured we'd all get back to our regular lives, at long last.

Looming above us, however, was Dr. Lee's warning. At our first meeting with her, she told us something I've never forgotten: "Prepare yourself for failure."

We didn't know these stats at the time—and most private places aren't eager to share them, either—but industry-standard success rates for overcoming substance abuse are somewhere between 10 and 25 percent. What does that tell you? Three out of every four people, at least, will fail. Dr. Lee was being realistic, and preparing us for the most likely outcome.

But of course we didn't want to believe Bruce would wind up in that overwhelming majority—in part because we were willing to shell out whatever money was required to fix the problem. At the time, we still believed it was a relatively simple fix: go into treatment sick, come back home cured. We didn't understand that addiction is like cancer. You might think it's gone for good, but there's no guarantee it won't come back when you least expect it.

The fact is, nobody wants to believe that their loved one will wind up in the overwhelming majority of cases where recovery doesn't last. Everyone wants to believe their family is the exception to the rule. Unfortunately, the math doesn't lie.

• • •

Our first call from the treatment centre staff came a lot sooner than we'd hoped. On his third day there, they called to tell us that the previous evening, Bruce had had a panic attack. They didn't tell us much more—just that it had happened, and that they were able to calm him down and get him back on track.

A week later, we got a second call. While living at the treatment centre, residents had some privileges, one of which was that they could walk to a gas station across the street to buy a cup of coffee or a snack. Bruce, however, decided to go there and buy Gravol—as a way, I can only assume, of treating his withdrawal symptoms. But having other drugs in his system was a clear violation of the rules, and this time the staff were calling me to say that Bruce would have to leave the centre for a couple of days.

Suffice to say, this was not what we wanted to hear. I told the person on the phone, "You can't do that to him. Where is he supposed to go? The whole point of this was to get him out of Winnipeg."

But they were still determined to kick him out, and so I had to reach out to a criminal lawyer I knew in Vancouver who'd defended a lot of gang members over the years. (He also happens to be my best friend's brother.) He wrote a letter to the centre laying out the reasons that Bruce's life would truly be in danger if he was forced to come back to Winnipeg, and eventually the centre relented and agreed to keep him.

That didn't absolve Bruce of his responsibility, of course. He knew the rule he was breaking. They were clear up front: when you go into treatment, you're not allowed to take *anything*. But he'd decided to take a chance anyway, the way he always did. And when you think about it, what's Gravol to a guy who was hard on the Oxys? What was that even meant to do? Anne and I were crestfallen. We realized Bruce must've been so desperate that he was willing to take anything that might help take the edge off.

Much more common than calls from the staff, however, were calls from Bruce himself. In fact, he called us pretty much every day, just to check in and tell us what he was up to and what was going on around the centre. And he called his girlfriend even more often than that. The two of them would have long (and expensive) conversations about all kinds of things—most often, about what they were going to do when he got out.

Bruce knew he wasn't going back to Winnipeg, at least for the time being. We thought it was in his best interest to stay away for a year or two, just so the drama with this gang member had time to blow over. In the meantime, Halifax seemed like a logical fit. It was about as far away as we could send him within Canada, plus he would have my parents nearby as a support system. Walt also had a lot of business connections in the area and offered to help find him a job. Everyone agreed it was a perfect opportunity for a second chance. But Bruce told us he would only do it if his girlfriend would agree to come with him, but we weren't so sure it was a wise idea.

About halfway through Bruce's time there, the treatment centre held a family weekend, where loved ones could come visit the centre, see how much progress their family members were making, and learn a bit more about what was involved in treatment and how to help once the program was over. Anne, Darcy, and I all flew out to see for ourselves how Bruce was doing.

We got there just after lunchtime, nervous and not exactly sure what to expect. When I first saw Bruce, I started crying on the spot. I was stunned at how much better he looked. This was the Bruce we always knew he could be: he'd regained all that lost weight, and the awful bags under his eyes were completely gone. He looked like he had during his most athletic days as a boxer, but now filled out into a man's build—no steroids required. Even better, he looked happy. It was a miraculous turnaround. Anne and I couldn't wait to hug him, and Darcy wasn't far behind.

As we walked around the centre with him, it was clear that Bruce was a popular guy there. He'd always been very social and outgoing, and inside he'd made friends with a lot of the other guys, in particular a couple of soldiers who were struggling with PTSD. They spent a lot of time together and became close. It was another positive sign about his ability to make a new life for himself.

The first thing we did as a family was take part in a big sharing circle. There were around a dozen families in the group, and the idea was we would go around, one by one, and tell the story of how our loved ones—it was mostly parents talking about their kids—had ended up in treatment. Anne and I were fourth in line, and I got really nervous. I remember thinking to myself, *Oh my God, our story is going to be the worst of them all—an assault with a club! What could be worse than that?*

But as soon as other people started sharing their stories, I started to reconsider. And by the time they got to us, I turned to Anne and whispered, "Hey, maybe we're actually not doing so bad!"

The stories we heard from these other families were intense, and spoke to the power of addiction in all of its many forms. One of the other kids in treatment had been cutting themselves. Another was a gambler who'd stolen and secretly sold a bunch of their family's personal possessions. Another was a sex addict. It was just an assortment of horrid experiences that these families had gone through—but, in a way, it reassured me that we weren't out of place in being there. Our story, it turned out, wasn't one in a million. Compared to some of the other ones we heard in that circle, it didn't even seem all that dramatic.

During family weekend we were also taught a series of coping exercises and strategies. These were meant to help us understand Bruce's mindset and help communicate with him more effectively once he was out of treatment, but I wasn't so sure. If I'm being totally honest, I thought it was bullshit. Nothing they told us seemed particularly helpful. We didn't learn anything, for instance, about how to deal with Bruce's dogged determination, which was the source of so many of our arguments. Instead, we did things like stand in a big group session and yell out crazy shit like, "I don't like it when you do that to me!" What kind of insight was *that* supposed to give us? I remember turning to Anne at one point and whispering, "What's the point of this again?" (Darcy, at least, had figured it out ahead of time, and he spent the entire second day back at our hotel.)

Our final memory of family weekend was another tough one. Anne and I ended up getting in a nasty argument with Bruce—and, to make it worse, it happened right in front of one of the counsellors. It was an argument we'd been having over the phone, in various forms, about whether his girlfriend should come with him to Halifax. Bruce told us, to our faces this time, that this was the only way he would agree to go. I don't know that she even wanted to go.

But over the course of those weeks of phone calls, she had eventually agreed to try.

Anne and I were strongly against the idea, because he and his girlfriend could be pretty toxic together, and because we wanted him to have as few ties to his past as possible in starting over. We also wanted Bruce to live, at least at first, in a designated sober-living house, where his roommates would be other people who were sober and in recovery and who could keep an eye on him. But, as usual, he pushed and pushed and pushed until Anne and I were both in tears. We just could not get through to him. He was immovable, and no amount of treatment was going to change that. So, we relented.

Still, Anne, Darcy, and I managed to fly back home to Winnipeg feeling positive overall. I held on to the belief that the staff at the centre knew what they were doing, and that everything would turn out okay in the end. Anne and I were relieved to see that Bruce was working hard, and we were optimistic he was going to get the best out of the experience and be able to get his life back on track once he got back out. What did it matter, really, if a couple of the exercises were a bit abstract?

When the six weeks were officially up, the treatment centre held a kind of graduation ceremony for everyone about to head back into the real world. This is common within the world of recovery, and is an opportunity for the counsellors to say a few words about each client, and for the clients themselves to give a short speech in front of an audience of their loved ones.

I wasn't able to be there, unfortunately, due to my usual work schedule I couldn't get out of it. But Anne went and reported back. As we would learn for ourselves later, these graduation speeches can be kind of all over the place, because some of the clients are downright terrified of public speaking, and don't get much out beyond mumbling, "Thanks, everyone." And that's fine; to each their own. But Bruce, outgoing guy that he was, absolutely stole the show. He got up on the microphone and gave a stirring speech that touched on all the people who'd helped him in his journey, and gave a particular shout-out to his new friends in the military. Anne was so proud, even in the retelling of the story. Bruce had always been really good at that sort of thing, and on the stage that day he really created the impression that he was ready to move on.

We hoped this experience would mark the end of Bruce's recovery journey. We had no idea we were still barely over the starting line.

Looking back on it, I think the problem with that private treatment centre was that it was staffed by people who were book-smart. They all had their degrees, and they were all up on the latest theories and literature and what have you. But as far as I know, none of the counsellors there had actually been through recovery themselves. And if you've never walked the walk, how can you really know what your clients are going through? It's kind of like in the NHL: there aren't a lot of coaches out there who haven't played the game at a pro level, because there's always that risk of one of their players turning around and saying, "Well, what do you know, anyway?" It's a similar thing in recovery. If you're going to look an addict in the eye and say, "I know what you're going through," you'd better have actually done it. And in this case I just don't think they had.

While I may have some complaints in hindsight, the truth is that the private treatment centre did exactly what they said they would.

We never felt like we'd thrown our $20,000 out the window or anything. Even when things started to go sideways again, we always considered it part of Bruce's journey. But as it turned out, this was a part of the journey that many of those in recovery end up making. I can't count how many stories I've heard over the years from guys who are on their third, fourth, or even fifth attempt at getting sober. It just seems to be the way it goes.

The difference with Bruce is that I believe he walked out of that building completely confident that he was cured. If there was one lesson that should've been imparted on him upon leaving treatment— and maybe it was, and he just chose to ignore it, I can't be sure—it is that you need to make the right choices going forward. You can't allow yourself to slip back into your old habits. If you want to have this healthy life you're imagining for yourself, you cannot drink or use drugs, ever again. Whereas Bruce, I know, ended up using again pretty well as soon as he was out of there. I just wish he'd left with a better understanding, or maybe a stronger desire, to stay sober for good.

But, look, it's addiction. And recovery is not linear. This I've come to know. If you've never had a loved one experience addiction, I can understand you might have a knee-jerk reaction to all of this: *They paid $20,000 for a fancy private centre, he should be fine! If not, what was all that money for?* But that just isn't how it works. The line of recovery might go straight ahead for a while, but then it can stop, or back up, or spiral or zig-zag or loop-de-loop, and then it does the whole thing all over again. You never really know what's coming next.

So it might sound a bit naïve, looking back on it, but we had such high hopes for Bruce. He seemed to be set up for a whole new life, yet it couldn't have gone more horribly wrong. As it turns out, opioids were much more readily available in port cities than they were in the interior of Canada. Less than a year after he arrived in Halifax, Bruce was a full-fledged IV heroin addict.

Critical Mass

After graduation, Bruce headed off to Nova Scotia to try to start over. For people who are newly sober, it's usually recommended that they move into what's called second-stage housing—in other words, a designated sober-living arrangement. That's what Bruce's counsellors suggested for him, and we managed to convince him to try it. Unfortunately, this arrangement didn't last long. But it wasn't all Bruce's fault. The place he'd been recommended turned out to be full of older guys who were recovering from alcoholism, and the only person his age was a guy named Richard. Within a couple of weeks he was on the phone to us again, complaining about his situation to no end.

"I don't have anything in common with these guys," he said. Plus, he was desperate to see his girlfriend again.

So yet again, it was Mom and Dad to the rescue. Anne flew out to Halifax and helped Bruce rent his own apartment. It was a one-bedroom in a low-rise building in a nice part of town, not far from the Bedford Basin. She then went around and bought a bunch of new furniture to furnish it with. It was all nicely set up—a lot nicer, all told, than the first apartment I ever had when I left home. The rent was around $600 per month, and Anne and I agreed to pay it for him until he got back on his feet.

My parents also did their best to help Bruce. Walt found him a nice used car, and also a job with a local dispatching company. It's funny how grandparents have a way with their grandchildren—it's like a second chance to get it right, and learn from the way you parented your own children. My parents may not have lived nearby, but they were always interested in Bruce's and Darcy's lives. And when Bruce's struggles began, that's all they wanted to hear about.

My parents knew he'd been a handful since a young age. When drugs entered the picture, that became an open topic of conversation between them and me, too. We discussed everything, including the assault. They were afraid for Bruce, like any grandparents would be, and they did their best to reassure Anne and me that things would work out. When the opportunity for him to live closer to them came up, they were happy to have the opportunity to get more involved and do whatever they could to help.

Then, once Bruce was settled, his girlfriend flew out and moved in with him, just like they'd been planning. It was a great opportunity for a fresh start, and Darcy even flew over early on to hang out and see how Bruce was doing. The two of them had always been close, and it meant a lot to me to see them putting in work to keep that sibling bond strong, even if they were now living thousands of kilometres apart. Darcy was a good influence on Bruce, and when he got back I was eager to hear how his older brother was doing. Darcy said Bruce was all right, but he didn't share many details. Looking back on it, I think he was again trying to balance being a responsible sibling with not being a tattletale. It was a tough balancing act, but Darcy did his best to manage it.

Unfortunately, our optimism about Bruce's fresh start quickly began to fade. The first sign came during our regular phone calls. By now we'd learned some of the signs of drug use to look for, and we noticed that he sometimes sounded strange over the phone. But when we'd ask what was going on, he would always give the same excuse: that he was groggy because he'd just woken up from a nap. Anne and I couldn't prove otherwise, of course, but we started to become concerned.

The second sign was when he lost his job at the transportation company, less than a month after he'd started it. Again, Bruce tried to brush this off as no big deal, but it certainly didn't seem like good news.

And the third sign came not long afterwards, when his girlfriend left—again, less than a month after she'd gotten there. It's hard to know what happened between them. My guess is that she never really wanted to be there to begin with, but Bruce had gradually managed to convince her. Once she had proof that the situation wasn't going to work, she moved on.

When Bruce called me and told me his girlfriend had left, we knew right away this could be a big turning point in his sobriety. Anne and I were at the cottage at the time, and he sounded heartbroken on the phone. We discussed the situation the entire drive back, and it was

Anne who first suggested that I go down there to be with him. I knew she was right. After all, it was the summertime, so my work schedule couldn't get in the way, the way it had so many times in the past. This time I could be there with Bruce as long as he needed me to be.

The next day, I got on a plane.

Bruce picked me up from the Halifax airport and brought me back to his apartment, where I discovered he wasn't on his own after all. Richard, from the second-stage housing, was there in Bruce's apartment, and it turned out he'd been staying on Bruce's couch to keep him company. Richard seemed like a nice guy, and I was glad to learn that Bruce had some kind of support network in the city to lean on.

Now that I was there, however, Richard decided to find somewhere else to stay. He asked for a ride to another friend's house, and when it was just the two of us in Bruce's car, he said, "Look, I've got to tell you something. Bruce is using again."

When he said those words, I felt like a stake was being driven through my heart. *Oh, God. Here we go again.*

It wasn't totally shocking news, so much as a confirmation of my worst fears and suspicions. Anne and I had wondered why Bruce always seemed so out of sorts on the phone. Now we knew. It explained a few other things, too, like why Bruce had been fired from his dispatching job so quickly. And why, a few weeks earlier, my mother had discovered a bunch of her medication had gone missing—right after Bruce came by for a visit.

As Richard and I were talking, it started to rain. By the time he got out of the car, it was a full-on rainstorm. I called Anne and told her the news.

"You should leave," she said, as upset and overwhelmed as I was. "Tell him he's on his own, and come home."

My head was spinning, so much so that I got lost on the drive back to Bruce's apartment. When I finally got there, Bruce still wasn't home from work. He didn't get back until around midnight, at which point my bag was already packed.

I confronted him about what Richard had told me, and, as always, he denied it. He said Richard was lying. I knew in my heart that wasn't the case, and Bruce's excuses made me even more angry. I felt like I was at my wits' end. I was just so frustrated at Bruce for breaking his end of the bargain. The promise of recovery, which we'd all fought so hard for, felt like it was slipping away. At the time I still didn't know much about addiction, so I didn't comprehend that I was blaming the victim. Yes, Bruce had relapsed. But Anne and I didn't understand how common this is in the world of recovery, and that the correct response is more patience, not less of it.

"If this is what you're going to do," I told him, "you are on your own."

I was really furious. But in the end, somehow, I didn't leave. In fact, I ended up staying for eight days in total.

Why? Despite my bluster in the heat of the moment, I knew I wasn't ready to give up on my son. And I knew what would happen if I left. By being there with him, I figured I could provide not just emotional support, but also some structure to his days. So I tried to make myself useful. I drove Bruce to a new job at a call centre—similar to what he'd done back home in Winnipeg—in part to make sure he actually went. And I helped him change the locks to his doors, because it turned out that Richard had stolen Bruce's Game Boy and a few other possessions on his way out. Richard also had a spare key to the apartment, which meant he could theoretically come back anytime.

I also took Bruce on another trip up to visit my parents in Amherst, where, I hoped, he could enjoy some quiet downtime with his grandparents. Despite our openness about Bruce's struggles, I didn't tell them about the relapse, figuring he would benefit more if he didn't feel like he was under their extra scrutiny, too. We went to the mall, ate lunch together, and watched TV. It was a nice, relaxing visit.

But on our way back, I was trying to get Bruce to attend a meeting that evening in Dartmouth, and we were running late. I drove as fast as humanly possible to get him there in time, at which point Bruce wandered in and sat there, completely unengaged and uninterested. He might as well have been watching the opera.

Anne and I had tried to take Dr. Lee's advice seriously. We'd tried to prepare ourselves for failure. But this was still a shock. Bruce was only a few months out of the private facility, and he seemed to be right back where he'd started. Was *this* the kind of failure she was talking about? I was thunderstruck. In retrospect, I probably shouldn't have been so surprised. Bruce had arrived in Halifax sober, but I don't think he had in any way worked on his sobriety since that point. One common piece of advice they tell you in the early stages of recovery is to attend 90 meetings in 90 days. Well, I don't think Bruce attended even one. I think he really believed he was cured, and on some level Anne and I did, too. Given that attitude, relapsing was an accident waiting to happen.

Looking back, I realize that Anne and I were trying to force recovery on him. And that never works. As parents, we kept hoping that the light would go on eventually—that one day Bruce would go to a meeting and hear a story that would make him realize he had to take this more seriously. But it's a misguided notion. When family members want the addict to be sober more than the addict themselves, it's a recipe to make everyone crazy.

I couldn't force Bruce to be sober and I couldn't stay in Halifax forever. After eight days I flew back home, where my other obligations and commitments were waiting for me. In the short term, at least, Bruce would have to fend for himself.

The next time Anne and I saw him was that fall in Calgary, where our godson Bret was getting married. Bret is the son of Mark and Debbie, our best friends, and he, Bruce, and Darcy had grown up together and were very close—to look at them you'd think they were all siblings.

I met up with the boys the night before the wedding and we went for dinner together. Bruce seemed okay, but I had my doubts. By this time he'd gotten yet another job out east, this time working in a warehouse loading trucks for a big grocery chain. It was a union job, with benefits, and it sounded like a great opportunity. I asked him how it was all going, and his answers were optimistic, but brief.

The real giveaway to his current state came the next day. Back in Amherst, my mother had taken Bruce to the local tailor and got him fitted with a nice suit. But now, when he showed up to the ceremony, the suit didn't fit him properly anymore. It was too big around the neck. I later mentioned this to my mother and she said it had fit perfectly when she bought it for him. That's how quickly he was losing weight from drugs.

After the ceremony, I had to duck out to the Saddledome to cover that night's Flames game for *Hockey Night in Canada*, but I planned to come back in time to join the reception at the hotel. When I got there, I couldn't find Bruce. I asked Darcy to see if he could find him, and it turned out Bruce was upstairs in one of Bret's friend's rooms. When Darcy walked in the door, Bruce had a drink in his hand.

That really upset me. I may not have known a lot about recovery, but I knew that you absolutely cannot drink alcohol. It has to be total abstinence. But again, I'd be lying if part of me didn't understand Bruce's thinking in that moment. He was an outgoing guy in his early twenties. Was he really unable to ever have a beer with his friends ever again?

It wasn't until after the wedding, when Bruce went back to Halifax, that we learned he'd already been fired from his job in the grocery warehouse. By this point his use was so bad that his inability to keep a job was twofold: the drugs made him unable to regularly show up to work, and they made him physically unfit to do the work on those times when he *did* make it in. It was another blow.

If I'm being honest, this period of Bruce's life is a bit of a blur. There were so many trips and rescue missions from Winnipeg to Halifax, it's hard to keep them all straight in my memory.

There was the time Anne and I discovered a pile of letters from the provincial government on his kitchen table because he'd been skipping out on a thousand dollars' worth of traffic tickets. (Anne wrote a cheque for that, despite my protests.)

There was the time I brought Bruce into his kitchen so I could check his arms for track marks under the bright fluorescent lights. (He didn't have any, but in retrospect I think it's because he was injecting between his toes instead.)

And there was the time—against all odds—that he showed up to Christmas at my parents' house in Amherst with a beautiful new girlfriend. She was from Peggy's Cove, and she was extremely nice. None of the rest of the family could believe Bruce's luck. How had he managed to land a girl like her? Unfortunately, she didn't know the first thing about drug use or how deep Bruce was in it, and so couldn't recognize how badly he was struggling.

After our Christmas festivities were done, his girlfriend went back home to see her family, and Bruce was once again alone in his apartment. Anne and I could tell he was only barely keeping it together while she was there, so we decided to follow him back to Halifax and try to get him into detox one last time. The night we arrived, he came by our hotel, and I asked if he was going to a meeting that night.

"Oh yes, don't worry," he assured me.

He left at around 8 p.m. and came back an hour later—nowhere near long enough to actually attend a meeting. More likely, he just went back to his apartment and waited around a bit to try to get one over on us. I was so fired up from him lying, again, that I had two or three glasses of wine to unwind before falling asleep.

The next morning, we went back to his apartment to take him to detox, whether he wanted to or not. It took twenty minutes, and multiple phone calls to get him down into the car, and it was another dramatic scene at the detox building, because Bruce was trying whatever he could think of to leave, while the staff were all but begging him to stay. I think they could tell how desperate we were. At one point Bruce went off to use the bathroom, but came back after only thirty seconds or so. By now this kind of behaviour was a red flag to me—and to the nurse, too. He probably snuck off to take an Oxy. From there the nurse really zeroed in on him, and made every argument she could to convince him to stay.

In the middle of this back-and-forth, she paused and said, "I smell alcohol, too. Have you also been drinking?" I realized whose breath the smell was coming off of, and had to jump in to say, "No, wait, that's me!"

More comedy amid the tragedy. In that moment there was a part of me that thought, *Is this how it ends? Am I going to end up in detox and Bruce isn't?*

Ultimately, we just couldn't convince him to stay. Bruce insisted he could do it on his own, and that this time it would work. Obviously, it wasn't true. But what other choice did we have?

By April, it was clear Bruce was in big trouble. We'd never stopped paying his rent, and on top of that there were now constant requests for short-term cash infusions. He'd call us and say he needed money for gas, or that his PlayStation was stolen out of his car and he needed a new one. Even at the time, I doubted most of that was true. I suspected his PlayStation was more likely in the pawn shop to settle a debt for more Oxys. Plus the quality of our conversations kept declining. Bruce was continually groggy on the phone, always insisting he'd just had a nap, no matter what time of day it was; if you took him at his word, he must've been sleeping around the clock. Anne decided to go out and try to convince him to go back to detox.

I couldn't go with her, because by now the Stanley Cup playoffs had started, and I was stuck flying back and forth between Pittsburgh and Ottawa to cover the Penguins and the Senators in the first round. This is the busiest time of year on the hockey calendar, and I still didn't feel like I could just up and leave in order to take care of my family. Very few of my coworkers at *Hockey Night in Canada* knew what was going on with Bruce, but one of the exceptions was a senior producer named Sherali Najak. Technically Sherali was my boss, but mostly the two of us were just good friends. He'd heard plenty of stories about the boys since they were young, and both Bruce and Darcy knew his penchant for pranks firsthand. Once he called Bruce and pretended to be an executive at some record label, and got him to rap for him over the phone. When Sherali finally burst out laughing, thereby giving away the joke, Bruce fumed, "I *knew* it was you!" Sherali had even visited Bruce when he was staying at the private treatment centre in Toronto, just to see how he was doing. He was a great source of friendship and support in those years, and I leaned on him yet again while Anne was with Bruce now.

The two of them drove to a small-town hospital in Nova Scotia, where a nurse asked Bruce, "What drugs are you using?" He turned around and sheepishly asked Anne to leave the room, because he didn't want her to hear that he'd graduated to heroin. It was confirmation of our worst fears, and an incredibly sad moment for both of them. From that point on, Bruce didn't even try to conceal the track marks on his arms from us.

Somehow, Bruce managed to make it through detox, and when that was done I was able to duck out between playoff series and join them, where Anne and I took Bruce straight into another private treatment facility. This one was in Nova Scotia, and it offered a thirty-day program that cost us around $7,000. Once again, we were happy to pay it.

I'm not sure what our expectations were for Bruce at this point. Anne and I had given up the idea that paying for fancy private treatment was a miracle cure—we'd learned the hard way that, when it comes to addiction, there's simply no such thing. It was clear this was going to be a longer, and more painful, journey than we'd previously believed. I think we were just trying everything we could think of. If the treatment centre in Toronto hadn't been what Bruce needed, maybe this one would be.

Unfortunately, it didn't turn out that way. This treatment centre was pretty small, with a limited number of beds, and all of the other residents were middle-aged alcoholics who didn't relate to Bruce, and vice versa. He completed his stay there, but I wasn't feeling optimistic about his long-term chances for sobriety—I'm pretty sure he was already using again before his thirty days were even up. Bruce went back to his apartment in Halifax, and when I called him a few days later, it was like nothing had changed. He sounded *exactly* as messed up on the phone as he had when Anne called him, months earlier. Even worse, he continued to trot out the same old excuse: he was groggy, he'd just woken up from a nap.

I was furious. I said to him, "You better get your ass back to that centre for their next meeting. And you better prepare to be drug tested."

In the meantime I called the treatment centre directly, looking for answers. I told them Bruce was already off the wagon and asked how that could have happened so quickly. They told me I was being too hard on him and that he needed some space, which didn't exactly fill me with hope.

Bruce, at least, did agree to go back to the centre for a meeting. While he was there, he also took a drug test. The problem was that I'd warned him it was coming, so he'd had time to prepare. That night I got a call from the treatment centre: the results from the urine sample came back negative. Bruce was clean. I thought, *There's no way. Something is going on here.*

It wasn't until months later that he told me the truth: it was someone else's piss. Bruce had used a trick that countless other addicts before him have tried. You acquire someone else's clean urine, put it in a condom, and tape it to your thigh to keep it warm. Then you go into the bathroom stall and pass it off as your own. This trick works, but it isn't foolproof: I've heard stories about addicts accidentally handing in urine samples that are still so cold, if it had actually come out of their bodies, they'd be dead. But Bruce was willing to take that chance, like always, and this time he'd managed to pull it off.

Despite Bruce's reassurances at the time, his situation was unravelling. And things came to a head again that summer, just as I was preparing for another big trip—this time to Beijing for the 2008 Olympics.

I was scheduled to fly over in late July, and had been assigned the same job I'd done at previous Olympics, which was being the host/reporter for aquatics and track and field. It was a lot of work to prepare for, and I was frayed emotionally.

The day before I left, Anne and I happened to attend the funeral of a classmate of Bruce's. They'd been friends, and, despite lives of privilege, both had been drawn into the gangster lifestyle. Unfortunately, this friend hadn't been as lucky as Bruce had: he'd become a drug dealer and ended up being brutally murdered. It was just an awful situation, and Anne and I were heartbroken for his family. The service was at a church in the West End of the city, and I sat there in my black suit, looking at his grieving parents and grandparents, and thought: *that's going to be us one day.* I cried at that funeral—both for the boy and for Bruce.

When I got back home that night, I finished up the rest of my packing, and was literally closing up my duffel bag when I got a call from my executive producer at CBC. He said, "I need you to do me a favour. I need you to do rowing, too."

"What do you mean, *do rowing?*"

"The guy who was supposed to do it can't come to China after all," the producer said. "He's sick. I want you to do it instead."

"Are you kidding?" I said. "I've never covered rowing in my life! Of all the regattas in the world, this would be my first. I can't *start* at the Olympics."

I tried to argue my case, but if you've ever had a boss, you know how these requests go. You can either do them willingly, or against your will. So I had no choice but to say okay.

I was supposed to be unwinding before bed, but now my mind was racing. Throughout my career, I've always had the same recurring thought: that I'm one show away from being found out as a total fraud. So now I figured, *This is it. This is how they finally get me.*

Despite the late hour, I called up my colleague Chris Cuthbert, who is one of the most talented broadcasters in the business, and who

I knew had done rowing at a number of previous Olympics. I told him about my new assignment, and the first words out of his mouth were, "Jesus, you're kidding!" That didn't fill me with confidence.

This was before YouTube had taken off, and we also didn't have time to arrange for him to send me DVDs of past Olympic regattas. But Chris agreed to send over as much material as he could via email, and in the meantime gave me a bunch of tips about how to call it and what to look for. I was desperate for whatever advice I could get.

The next morning, I headed to the airport, where my flight was from Winnipeg to Vancouver, and then connecting from there to Beijing. During my layover in Vancouver, I called Bruce to check in, and this time he couldn't even pretend: he was totally fucked up. At this point he was buying heroin from someone who claimed that Bruce owed him money, a claim that Bruce said wasn't true. "And when I see that guy," he said, slurring his words, "I'm going to stab him in the neck."

On the one hand this was typical addict nonsense, obsessing over who did what to whom. But even if Bruce was exaggerating, the tone of the whole conversation terrified me. He was clearly not functioning properly. I thought: *what am I doing? I can't go to China at a time like this.*

I called Anne to tell her what was going on, and she said not to worry, that of course I should go, and that she would take care of things while I was gone. She was right, but I still felt like I was going in the exact opposite direction of where I needed to be. That flight to Beijing was thirteen hours long, and I spent the first hour reviewing all of my rowing material. The next twelve I spent worried sick about Bruce.

Once I arrived in China, I tried to refocus on the details of my new favourite sport. As it turned out, the guy I was covering rowing with, an Olympic silver medallist named Barney Williams, was doing TV for the first time, so he was just as nervous as I was. We did a couple of dry runs together in the broadcast centre, and eventually started feeling more comfortable. Thankfully, once we were on the air, Barney carried me through the event itself.

Whenever I had a free moment, I called home to see how things were going. It just so happened that my mother and sister were in Manitoba, staying at the cottage with Anne, and their updates seemed promising. It wasn't until the last day of the trip that Anne levelled with me.

"Bruce isn't fine," she admitted on the phone. "He's off the rails. We need to do something."

It was a parallel to the days following Bruce's assault by the drug dealer. In the same way that I'd tried to protect Anne from the truth in order to get through my mother's birthday weekend, she had shielded Bruce's current state from me so that I could get through my Olympics assignments without becoming a nervous wreck. This was just another example of the way that Anne and I were always on the same wavelength, and always looking out for one another in times of stress.

Finally, we'd reached critical mass. It had become painfully obvious to Anne and me that the short-term stuff wasn't working. All the time and money we'd spent trying to bail Bruce out wasn't helping him. In fact, it might have been doing the opposite. When I got back from Beijing, we sat down together to talk things through, and once again came to the same conclusion: it was time to try something different.

But now, when I tried to reach him, I couldn't. He wouldn't even answer his phone. So I had to resort to sending Bruce texts. I told him: *That's it. We're done. No more money from us. We are finished. The best offer you're going to get is: if you get yourself to detox, we'll help you find a long-term treatment/sober-living situation.*

Anne stood over my shoulder as I typed out the message. I looked up at her, she nodded, and I pressed send.

We finally got Bruce on the phone the next day, and he pleaded with us to reconsider.

"I can do it on my own," he insisted. "I can get this straightened out without detox."

But we held firm.

"No, you can't," I told him. "You've proven that you can't. We're well past that point now. This is our last and best offer, Bruce. I suggest you take it."

The next night, he called us again and told us that he was so broke, he'd resorted to eating cat food. Anne dissolved into tears and passed me the phone. But I could see what he was doing: pulling at our heartstrings, like always.

I told him, "You know, Bruce, some seniors have had to eat cat food during hard times and they've all survived. So can you."

I managed to keep my hard-ass tone of voice just long enough to hang up the phone. Then I started to cry, too, and turned to Anne.

"Fuck it," I said. "We've got to stick to our guns here."

She looked at me with tears still in her eyes. "You're right. We have to try."

Miraculously, this new approach actually seemed to work. The very next day, Bruce took himself to detox in Dartmouth, and he stayed there for nearly two weeks. It wasn't easy for him—at one point he told the staff he was thinking about leaving, and I had to write a sternly worded fax to keep him motivated to stay—but he did it.

True to our word, Anne and I started looking into treatment centres as the next step. Bruce's godmother told us about a place in Calgary called Simon House that sounded promising, and I just so happened to have to go to Calgary anyway for an equestrian event. So I stopped by the facility and got a tour. They told me that one of the things that makes Simon House stand out is that all of their counsellors were in recovery themselves. I liked the sound of that.

From there it happened quickly. They did an intake interview with Bruce from the detox centre in Halifax, and then Anne and her friend Brenda went down to get him and close up his apartment. When the two of them opened the front door, they were horrified. It wasn't that the apartment was filthy—it's that it was empty. Everything of value had been sold or given away. Meanwhile, his car, which my father had given him, was full of needles and other drug paraphernalia. It was an upsetting scene, and Anne was just grateful to have a friend as good as Brenda there with her.

There was also a brief dispute about some unpaid rent. Anne spoke with the landlord directly, and told him, "Listen, you're getting rid of someone you probably wanted to throw out anyway." They saw her way of thinking, and agreed to let Bruce out of the remainder of his lease, no questions asked. When that was settled, the two of them brought Bruce up to Amherst, where I met him, picked him up, and brought him straight to Calgary.

In this case, the tough-love approach won out. But we also got lucky, in a way. The truth is, Anne and I were out of options. If we

kept enabling Bruce the way we had been, we figured he was probably going to wind up dead. At the same time, I also believe that if
we'd tried that same approach earlier, it wouldn't have worked. Bruce
wouldn't have been ready to hear it. Like a lot of addicts, he eventually found himself out of options, too. He had no job and no money.
What was he going to do, really?

From where we were standing, Simon House looked like a god-
send. On the day Bruce got there, the staff basically took one look at
him and said, *We're onto your bullshit.* The counsellors knew all the
tricks an addict could pull, and they weren't fooled by any of them.

Once again, a sense of peace came upon our home in Winnipeg.
Even when Bruce was in the private treatment centre in Toronto,
there were constant phone calls between us. At Simon House, however, they specifically told us *not* to call for a while, in order to let
Bruce find his own footing. So we didn't—and we didn't hear from
him for an entire month.

When I finally broke down and called Simon House, it was mostly
just to ask, "So, uh . . . Bruce is still there, right?"

"Oh, yes," the counsellor replied. "And he's doing great."

Caught in the Cycle

On our flights from Halifax to Calgary, Bruce told me he welcomed the opportunity in front of him—more than that, he admitted that he needed it. Looking at the track marks that covered both of his arms, I was glad to hear him say this. Of course, I'd heard him express some version of this sentiment before, more than once, and it had never ended well. But this time Anne and I once again found reason to hope. Bruce had hit rock bottom during the whole cat food episode, and I think he'd gained enough perspective to realize that he didn't want to spend all day long in drug-seeking behaviour anymore. To that end, he'd just finished two good weeks in detox, and the staff there even agreed to keep him a couple of extra days, because they knew he was going straight into long-term treatment. That success led me to think that we had a real shot here.

When Bruce and I walked in the front doors, I was struck right away by how different of a vibe there was at Simon House compared to the private treatment centre he'd been to in Toronto. For one thing, it was a much smaller operation and felt much more personalized. For another, it was located smack in the middle of a residential area in the city's Northwest—not just that, it really seemed to be integrated into the surrounding community. Here, Bruce wouldn't feel hidden away from the public, which is important in recovery. Living among neighbours matters. Feeling included and welcomed matters. So that was definitely appealing.

The building itself was gorgeous, too. The founders of Simon House had run a multimillion-dollar fundraising campaign to get the centre built, and they ended up exceeding their goal. That's how much support they had from the community. As a result, they had not just a main thirty-bed building that was new and modern but also a pair of duplex cottages that they used for designated second-stage living.

Simon House's biggest selling point, however, was that its counsellors had all been through recovery themselves. They'd actually lived the life, and weren't just repeating things they'd heard in a classroom. That meant they knew firsthand what Bruce was going through, and what he'd had to deal with just to get to this point of his recovery journey. It was a warm and empathetic atmosphere where it felt like everyone was on the same page.

Bruce and I took a quick tour of the building, and inside it seemed like a similar setup to Toronto. The facilities looked good, and Bruce's bedroom, which he would again share with a roommate, was clean and comfortable.

Looking around, the other clients seemed to skew much younger than they had at the treatment centres in the Maritimes, which made me think Bruce might have an easier time making friends and fitting in. Simon House only accepted men, and most of the guys there came from within Alberta. But they would take people from anywhere, so long as you met all the criteria and were willing to do the work.

By this point, Anne and I had already put a small fortune into getting Bruce treatment, so out of habit, I had my chequebook at the ready. "How much?" I asked, ready to write in whatever number they told me.

"Oh no, you don't pay here," the staff member said.

I recoiled in my chair. *Huh?*

It turned out that Simon House followed an unusual payment model, in which you don't actually spend any money up front. Instead, Bruce would register for provincial income support, and that monthly amount was then passed on to Simon House to help cover the cost of his bed. The intention was to make treatment as accessible as possible to folks who otherwise couldn't afford it.

Now, obviously the meagre amount a person gets from income support wasn't nearly enough to cover the actual costs incurred at a cutting-edge treatment centre, so Simon House also accepted donations—from clients and their families, as well as the general public—to make up the difference. (Anne and I, of course, were happy to make a few such donations over the coming months.) But that philosophy, which prioritized the addict's well-being above all else, was a complete 180-degree reversal from how we'd seen other private treatment centres operate. It was an incredibly reassuring thing to be part of.

Simon House ran their program in three phases. In phase one, you live in the main building and you go through treatment in close consultation with their counsellors. Once those staff decide you're ready for phase two, you move into one of their secondary houses, which are still on-site but come with fewer restrictions and more freedoms. And phase three is when you head back out into the world and return to your previous life, living sober but otherwise pretty much restriction-free.

Before I left, Bruce and I stood at the front doors of the centre and I told him, "It's time to do the work. Take advantage of this situation."

"I will," he said. And I believed him.

During the entire first month Bruce was there, we didn't hear from him once. In fact, during his first ninety days in Simon House, I don't think we spoke on the phone more than a handful of times. The reason for this was twofold: one, Bruce needed time on his own to work on his recovery, and two, the rest of us were slowly trying to reacquaint ourselves with our old lives.

The feeling during that first month, especially, was relief. Again, because now we knew where Bruce was, we knew he was safe, and we knew he was trying to get better. Anne read a bunch of books about addiction over the years, and in one of them, a mother wrote that one year she was so happy her daughter got into Harvard, and the next year she was happy that she was in jail. That's exactly how we felt. As a parent, you always want to know that your kid is safe. And being in treatment meant Bruce was more than safe. Now he had the prospect of a better, sober life.

Meanwhile, the rest of us settled back into our normal routines. I was fully into the NHL beat, travelling across Western Canada every Friday for the late game on *Hockey Night in Canada* and returning home bright and early every Sunday morning. Anne was doing her work as a part-time palliative care nurse for the Winnipeg Regional Health Authority. And Darcy was coming into his own in a totally different field: magic.

This wasn't always the plan. Darcy has always had a lot of natural athletic ability, and as a young kid he logged countless hours at the Pan Am Diving Club. He was even identified as a future prospect for competitive diving, but lost interest, as he put it, "when the yelling started." (I recently found a diving journal Darcy kept from these years. There was only one entry, in which he called one of his coaches a name I won't repeat here.) So he quit.

Instead, at age ten, he joined his school juggling club. Then he decided he wanted to buy a unicycle, and saved up all his money until he could afford to buy one. From there it was only a short step to joining the Winnipeg Magic Club, where he learned the basics, won a couple of contests, and started advertising his services for birthday parties around the city.

Anne or I would drive Darcy to these early gigs, and they seemed to go well. He didn't make a lot of money, but word got around, and before long he'd hooked up with a local booking agency. People would call the agency and say, "We have $1,000 for our company Christmas party. What would you recommend?"

The agent would reply, "Oh, we have this great magician!"

The person would agree, then have to hide their disbelief when a thirteen-year-old showed up to the function with one of his parents. But Darcy was so talented, even at that young age, that the audience would inevitably be blown away by his performance. He was a perfectionist, even then.

Like his brother, Darcy couldn't be deterred once he set his mind on something. After graduating high school in 2005, he went on to take probably a dozen minimum-wage jobs to supplement his magic gigs, and he either quit or got fired from (mostly the latter) every single one of them because they couldn't hold his attention. One of the more memorable jobs was his brief stint as a bartender at a hotel in downtown Winnipeg, where Darcy was fired because he kept giving free drinks to the attractive young hairdressers who were also his regular customers.

When Bruce moved out of the house, it wasn't long before Darcy took over the basement and filled it with all of his magic paraphernalia. He had such a passion for it that, at one point, we had twelve doves in the basement, three parakeets upstairs, and two Peking ducks in the backyard. Our poor pet pug spent all day trying to claw his way through the patio door to get to those ducks. The doves, meanwhile, moulted so badly that we had to change our furnace filter every couple of weeks, and eventually the furnace itself gave out completely. It was madness. One day he'd be accidentally burning the carpet when his fire routine went awry, and another he'd be unplugging the freezer so he could test out his theatre-grade music system. In that latter case, you can probably guess what happened next. Flash forward to Grey Cup Sunday two weeks later, and Anne opens the freezer to discover a thousand bucks' worth of meat sitting there, fully rotten. Darcy had forgotten to plug the freezer back in.

I look back on all that now and shake my head. At times it felt like we'd traded one kind of chaos for another. But those years were basically Darcy's self-education, because magic ended up paying off for him big-time. A few years later, he was doing a show in Paris when he was invited to appear on the reality-TV show *Britain's Got Talent*. He was reluctant, because magicians generally don't do well on shows like that, but he ended up wowing the judges and made it all the way to the finals. From there Darcy's career in the U.K. really took off—he wrote a book, *Behind the Illusion*, and even performed in Windsor Castle for Queen Elizabeth on her ninetieth birthday. So I guess all those extra furnace filters were, in the end, worth it.

All three of us had the freedom to do this because we were secure in the knowledge that Bruce was trying to get better. It was a totally different feeling than during his time in that apartment in Halifax, where pretty much every time the phone rang there was some new disaster to clean up. Thanks to Simon House, we were allowed to get back to the rest of our lives.

Once Bruce had been in treatment for ninety days, he got his first sobriety chip. These little metal tokens are meant to celebrate different milestones, and they're common in the world of recovery. The first ones originated within Alcoholics Anonymous, in the U.S., but have since been adopted by lots of twelve-step programs around the world. The one Bruce received for three months of sobriety was blue, and had the well-known serenity prayer written on the back: *God grant me the serenity to accept the things I cannot change, courage to change the things I can, and the wisdom to know the difference.*

Getting a chip is a big deal, because three months sober for an IV drug user can feel like three years. To celebrate Bruce's accomplishment, I wrote him a letter—which I later saw pinned to his wall when I went to visit. In it, I said, "Of all the things you've done in your life, this makes me the proudest." We knew how hard it had been for him to get there, and the hold that his addiction had had over him up to that point.

From there, though, it wasn't all smooth sailing. As I mentioned, Simon House has a three-phase system, and I think Bruce might've set a record for how long he stayed in phase one—ten months in total. But it wasn't for lack of interest on his part. In fact, Bruce was pretty much desperate to get to phase two, because he wanted the extra freedoms that came with it. There was a counsellor there who once joked to me that Bruce's middle name should've been When-Am-I. That's how often he wanted updates on when it would finally be his time to move on.

Generally, this decision is up to the discretion of the counsellors. By this point Bruce had stayed sober, and no longer appeared to be experiencing any physical symptoms of withdrawal. The cravings, for instance, would have been pretty much gone. Instead, it was more of a mental check. The staff need to know that the person is ready for the next challenge, and that they are ready for a new level of responsibility. Are they capable of living on their own? Can they manage their own time responsibly, or will they fall back into old habits? Are

they ready to reenter the world of romantic relationships, which can turn everything sideways? Bruce's age also probably played a role in their thought process. People in their early twenties simply have less experience being independent, and so tend to need more supervision in early recovery.

Eventually, however, Bruce got his wish. He graduated to phase two in the summertime, and as part of this transition, he was required to get a job. Simon House helped him get hired at a Foot Locker in a nearby mall, and he seemed to be doing fine at first. But within a few weeks, his old habits started to creep back in yet again.

As it was explained to me later, Bruce met some people at work who smoked dope together, and one day they invited Bruce to join them. Which he did. Unfortunately, someone from Simon House happened to see him while he was doing it and reported him. He was ordered to take another urine test, and this time it came back positive. So he had to leave.

The rules are somewhat different now, but back then Simon House was very punitive. If you screwed up, you were out. The way they saw it, if you couldn't make the most of your opportunity, they had plenty of other people on their waitlist who would. I don't think you were even allowed back on their property for a full calendar year after your offense. Anne and I disagreed with this philosophy, but we never complained about it. We knew what we signed up for. Bruce did, too.

Still, it was a terrible day the day he got kicked out. At first Bruce tried to tell us that it was because he'd gotten in a fight with someone, but I didn't believe that story for a minute. It was a deep enough routine by now that we knew Bruce would say anything to avoid the truth about his addiction—especially when it came to reasons why he'd gone off track. When the real story finally came out, Anne and I felt sick to our stomachs. It felt like everything we'd carefully built up had come crashing back down again. Bruce had barely managed to escape a bad situation in Halifax, and now we were scared he was going right back to that level.

The last few years of Bruce's life were spent caught in the same cycle that a lot of addicts find themselves. Active addiction, recovery, relapse. Active addiction, recovery, relapse. Over and over again. Anne and I had hope during those eleven months he was at Simon House that things would change, but then it was right back into the rest of the cycle. Every time we thought he'd finally escaped, Bruce got sucked back in.

Looking back, I suppose there were more warning signs that all wasn't well, even at Simon House. Bruce had come home for two visits while he was there, one for Christmas and another early in the summer of 2009. During both of those trips he seemed to be doing really well. He looked good and sounded good. As part of his treatment, he was working his way through the twelve steps of recovery, one of which is that you make amends and apologize to the people whose lives you've made miserable.

Well, Bruce's version of this was to quickly ask me one day, "So you forgive me, right?" We were playing backgammon together, and the question caught me off guard.

"Of course," I said.

And that was it.

Typically, you'd expect to hear a more sincere apology—or at the very least a longer one. I didn't get that, and when we discussed

it that night, it turned out Anne's apology hadn't been much better. Nor did we get a promise that things would be different going forward. It turned out to be one more sign that Bruce still hadn't fully bought into what recovery meant in the long term. Sure enough, he was kicked out just a few months after that second trip.

After leaving Simon House, Bruce was left on his own to figure things out. He moved in with a guy who he'd met earlier at Simon House, then moved on to another place with a pair of roommates—good guys, from what I could tell—who helped find him another job. This time Bruce was working in sales for a branch of the World Health chain of gyms, and he quickly became one of that location's top salespeople. This was kind of a surprise, to be honest, given everything else that was going on in his life. But again, Bruce was never short on charm.

The next time the four of us were all together was at Christmas. Physically, he looked okay, but it was obvious to everyone that Bruce was really struggling on the inside. He was antsy and agitated. The first thing he did was open the family fridge, spy one of those ready-made Caesars in a can, and down it instantly, without a second thought. He'd been using again, and he clearly needed something to take the edge off. I guess his plan was to stay clean while he was at home, but it wasn't that easy.

For years our family had volunteered at a local homeless shelter in Winnipeg, but this time, while the rest of us were serving lunch, Bruce had to go into another room and lie down. He was edgy and antsy, yet down at the same time. It was hard to watch.

Then, when he went back to Calgary, Bruce took all of the money he'd gotten as gifts and promptly blew it on drugs.

It was more frustrating, upsetting news, and from there the cycle just continued.

Bruce went back for another trip to detox, this time at a place called Renfrew in Calgary. These detox trips were tricky, though, because while Bruce would agree to go—on some level I think he knew he had to—it was never his idea. He could never recognize how bad the problem had become on his own.

Thankfully, in Calgary he had a friend named Jill, who was in recovery herself, and who did her best to help Bruce along. She took him with her to meetings, and helped convince him when it was time to go back to detox. Jill also took time to call Anne and me every so often to update us on how Bruce was doing, which we really appreciated.

In the summer of 2010, I was assigned to work that year's Calgary Stampede, and we convinced Bruce to come back home with me for a couple of weeks. I met him at the airport, and my first impression was that he actually looked pretty good. I think I even managed to convince myself he might be clean. But those hopes faded quickly—we hadn't even arrived at the cottage yet when his energy levels fell right off, and even finishing the commute was a major struggle for him. Bruce spent most of his time sleeping. It wasn't the kind of visit we'd hoped for.

The day Bruce got back into Simon House was one of the happiest days of our lives. It was the end of January 2011, and I'd been down in Raleigh, North Carolina, to work the NHL All-Star Game. On my way back home, I had a phone call with Simon House's executive director, who confirmed that Bruce had completed another stint in detox at Renfrew and would be officially returning to the centre the following week.

Anne and I didn't want to get too far ahead of ourselves, but this was really exciting. He was going to get a second crack at recovery, and in a place where he'd flourished the last time. This time it was Anne who flew out to be with him at drop-off. But on the drive over to Simon House, Bruce told her they had to make a stop first: he needed to get his eyebrows waxed.

Can you believe that? Bruce had always been a good-looking kid, and even during his worst moments, he was always concerned about his physical appearance. Anne agreed, but we both had a good laugh about it afterwards. Whatever else was going on in our lives, we always managed to find the humour in the situation—in times like this, we needed to.

So in he went again. This time, however, Bruce had trouble focusing on his sobriety. Instead, he became fixated on the fact that he didn't have easy access to his car. Suddenly he decided he needed it, right this minute. He called me to tell me so, and when I replied that I didn't think it should be a priority for him, that dogged determination of his reared its head again. "It's so I can take guys to meetings!" he claimed. Eventually, one last time, we gave in, and arranged to have the car parked on-site at Simon House.

It was a mistake. That car gave Bruce way too much freedom, way too quickly. Soon afterwards, he and another guy in Simon

House were secretly using together. The staff figured out something was off right away, and gave them both another round of urine tests. Both failed. Which meant both had to leave.

Bruce had returned to Simon House in February, and was kicked out for the second time on March 24, 2011. It was the beginning of the end.

The End

As soon as he got back on the streets again, Bruce went on a tear. Whatever he had on him, he was using. He was also driving around Calgary with a buddy of his, making drops for their shared dealer, which I guess is how he was getting his drugs in the first place.

The end began with another phone call. Anne and I were in Amherst visiting my parents, and Jill called to tell us that Bruce had been in an accident and hit a barrier on a bridge near Rockyview Hospital. The vehicle itself was a write-off, but miraculously Bruce hadn't broken any bones and wasn't even seriously injured. He was taken to the hospital anyway as a precaution, and sat around in Emergency for a few hours, but discharged himself before he could be checked out by a doctor—but not before going to the hospital bathroom and using the rest of the drugs he had on him at the time. Jill and her husband had a three-month-old baby at the time, so Bruce couldn't stay with them. But she came to pick him up from the hospital anyway, and instead dropped him off at his latest girlfriend's place.

Once he got there, Bruce proceeded to go straight into the girlfriend's bathroom and locked the door. He needed to shoot up again. His girlfriend figured out what was going on and yelled at him through the door, telling him he couldn't do that there. She actually called the cops on him, who showed up and tried to reason with him. Irritated, Bruce took off and instead wandered down to a nearby bar, just off the main drag on 16 Avenue NW. Bruce went into the men's bathroom there, locked himself in a stall, sat on the toilet seat, shot up, and overdosed.

When word got around the bar what had happened, an employee (who happened to be training to be a paramedic) climbed into the stall and got Bruce—who still had the needle hanging out of his arm—down onto the floor. The employee worked on him for a while, trying to get his heart beating again. The cops and the actual paramedics got there not long afterwards, but it was too late. Bruce was declared dead in the morning hours of March 28.

My cell phone rang in Amherst at around eight that morning. Anne and I were both asleep, and my phone was on her side of the bed, so she answered it. On the other end was a guy named Gord Hudson, who was a sergeant in the Winnipeg Police Service, and who I knew through his wife, Janice, who was a concierge at Air Canada. At the time he was working in the police's communications division, and when he'd showed up to work that day, he saw there was a notice of death for a twenty-five-year-old named Bruce Oake. The death had occurred in Calgary, but nobody had been able to notify his next of kin in Winnipeg.

Anne handed me the phone.

"Scott," Gord said gently, "this is a hard phone call. Have you heard about Bruce?"

"Yeah," I said, instantly wide awake, "he had a car accident. But he's okay, right?"

"Well, no. He's—gone. He's dead."

The words he was saying simply didn't register. In fact, my initial response was that Gord must be mistaken. I asked him outright: was he sure he didn't have his wires crossed with the news about the accident? Could there possibly be another explanation? I was stumbling and stammering, looking for any way out of what he had told me.

To Gord's credit, he agreed to check again. But I think he knew it was just a formality. He said he'd call back, and hung up.

The next three minutes felt like they passed in slow motion. I was still praying there had been some kind of miscommunication. But on the other hand, Anne and I always knew this call was a possibility. I felt a horrible sinking feeling in my gut that only got worse with each passing second.

Finally, Gord came back on the line and confirmed that no, he wasn't mistaken. The news was true. I put my hand over the receiver of the phone and said to Anne, "He's dead."

She just started screaming.

We'd tried to prepare ourselves over the years for this situation, but now that it was here, the reality was even worse than we could have imagined. I was completely overwhelmed and in shock. It was like I'd been hit by a tidal wave.

Partly it was the speed at which it had all fallen apart. Literally one week earlier, Bruce was safe in Simon House. We didn't know he'd secretly started using again, but I'd been worried about him all the same.

I thought back to the last time I saw him. It was just before he was kicked out for the second time. I was doing a game in Calgary and he came to meet me for breakfast at the Westin Hotel. He was telling me how he didn't know whether Simon House was the right place for him after all, and how maybe he wasn't going to stay there much longer. I remember thinking, *I don't like the sound of that*. I knew that people in recovery have good days and bad days, and maybe this was just one of Bruce's bad days, so I let it go. A couple of days later, he was on the street.

The truth is, every time an addict uses, they are rolling the dice with their life. And when you're talking about slamming heroin into your arm, the odds become even riskier. I remember I was once furious at Bruce for something he'd done in Halifax, and after hanging up the phone, I said to Anne, "Jesus Christ, this is not going to end until he's dead." It was always a possibility. And now it was our reality.

The news had barely begun to sink in when Anne said to me, "We need to get ahead of this."

We knew how quickly news like this could spread. In particular, we saw that word of his death had already reached the rap-battle network Bruce had once been part of, and they were posting about it on social media. Anne was worried that Darcy might read one of those messages, so she called him on the phone.

She hadn't even gotten the full sentence out when Darcy realized what was coming. All he could say was, "Mom, no."

From there, Anne and I tried to get ourselves together enough to start figuring out what else needed doing. I broke the news to my parents, and Gord's wife, Janice, graciously arranged our travel back to Calgary to bring him home. Darcy also flew out to meet us there, as did our godson Bret, whose wedding Bruce was at. They met us at the Air Canada Lounge in Calgary, and as soon as I saw Darcy in person I burst out in tears. (Anne whispered to me that people were staring. I whispered back, "I don't give a fuck!") Darcy had tears in his eyes, too, but he was doing his best to hold it together.

In that moment my heart went out to him. I'd lost a son, and he had lost his only brother.

In those early days, I was amazed at how brave Anne was through it all. I think it went back to her training as a nurse, especially in palliative care. She had practice staying focused in difficult situations. She was the one who went into the room at the funeral home in Calgary to spend a final few minutes with Bruce, and to cut off a few locks of his hair so that we could keep it with us. Darcy and I couldn't bring ourselves to go in that room, but she did.

In Calgary, we all stayed at the home of Mark and Debbie, and started making arrangements. It turns out there is a lot to attend to when a family member dies. First, Anne, Darcy, Bret, and I went to the funeral home, where we arranged for the cremation of Bruce's body and bought the urn that would hold his remains. Then there were the phone calls. I called the bank to get Bruce's bank account closed, and then the impound lot, where his busted-up car had been sitting since the crash. It was an awful, seemingly never-ending experience. Everyone we spoke to first asked for a death certificate, which at the time infuriated me. "I'm telling you he's dead," I'd say over the phone. "Is that not good enough?" In time I came to understand that, as harsh as it sounds, that's simply part of doing business.

I then managed to call up the police officer who was on the scene that night, who was a very compassionate guy and gave me some more details on what happened. Anne and I also arranged to meet up with Bruce's girlfriend and one of his former roommates, whom he'd lived with after being out of Simon House for the first time. We told them that Bruce's death wasn't their fault, and that we were just grateful for all they'd done in trying to help him.

That Saturday, I was in no shape to be working, and so took the weekend off to be back at home with Anne, Darcy, and a handful of our close friends. I knew my coworkers were planning to do something in Bruce's memory, so we tuned into *Hockey Night in Canada* together. As soon as the title sequence finished, and before any mention of that night's games, Ron MacLean delivered a wonderful spoken tribute to Bruce.

Then he played a clip of Bruce at the age of ten, giving a speech on my behalf at the Manitoba Sportswriters and Sportscasters annual dinner, at which I was to be inducted into the media wing of the Manitoba Sports Hall of Fame. I couldn't attend in person because I was off in Europe covering a World Cup ski race, and so little Bruce had stepped up to the mic on my behalf. "Even though I'm only ten years old, I understand the meaning of this honour," he told the crowd of hundreds. "That anyone in our family should be put into the hall of fame just for talking makes perfect sense." Then, during the opening of the second game, the editors took one of Bruce's rather graphic rap songs and—skilfully editing around the obscenities—used it as a soundtrack.

Even though I knew it was coming, the tribute was really emotional. All of us, quite frankly, were bawling in the living room. We'd been trying our best to keep things together, but to see Bruce on our TV screen that night, already controlling a room at the age of ten—it was hard not to think of all the possibilities in his life at that point, and what he could've been. Instead, he was dead. It didn't seem fair.

A few days later, we held a small private service in Bruce's memory at our home. Anne's uncle Jim was there, along with her brother and his wife. My brother Stuart and his wife were there, too. I'd asked Floyd Perras, who was then executive director of Solo Mission, the homeless shelter Anne and I volunteered at, to give a brief service, and it hit all the right notes. There were probably a dozen of us there in total, with Bruce's urn sitting in the middle, on the gate-leg table in the family room. That's where it would sit for years to come, next to the fresh flowers Anne would buy to place next to it every week.

By the following weekend, I was back at work. Because what else was I going to do? Coincidentally, my first game back was in Calgary, which was a bittersweet experience, to say the least. When I first stepped off the plane, I thought, *Is this a mistake? Should I even be here?* I spent a lot of time crying in my hotel room that weekend. But I also knew that work was a part of the routine I needed, and so I forced myself to get back on the air and get through it. On the drive back to the hotel from morning skate, my colleague Mark Lee, who was doing play-by-play that night, asked me some questions about Bruce, and I was grateful to have him there to listen to what I was going through.

As part of her own grieving process, Anne decided to fly back to Calgary a few months later to meet all of Bruce's friends in person, many for the first time. We'd received several phone calls from them following Bruce's death, and the friends all told us how guilty they felt about what had happened. This was understandable, but it was important to Anne to personally absolve them of any blame—including Bruce's girlfriend, who had told him not to shoot up in her apartment. She meant it, too. Both of us truly believed it was nobody's fault. When she saw them, Anne told his friends that the best thing they could do was carry on with their lives, because that's what Bruce would have wanted them to do.

She also decided she needed to see where Bruce had died for herself. She met up with her friend Debbie, and the two of them went back to the bar, where they convinced a server to take them into the men's room. Then they stood in front of that fateful bathroom stall and let the emotions wash over them. It turned out that the assistant manager who was working that day was also there on the night Bruce died. He came over to their table while Anne and Debbie were eating lunch afterwards and shared his memories about what he remembered from that evening.

And when their bill came, they saw the manager had given them a special discount—$8 off their lunch.

In the weeks and months to come, when Anne I started telling the story of Bruce's death, we always made a point of mentioning that detail. To us it was just so absurd—exactly the kind of black comedy that Bruce had loved. *That's the price for dying in a bathroom stall? Not seven bucks? Not nine? You can't just comp us the whole fucking meal?* Eventually we had to take the reference out, because nobody else seemed to find it funny. Or maybe they just weren't comfortable laughing at such a morbid joke, in the middle of such a sad story. But for the two of us, who were actually living that sad story, we were willing to take any moment of levity we could find.

But underneath her brave exterior, I came to realize that Anne was having a harder time than she let on. Within a few months of Bruce's death she told me she wanted to quit her job, and she started taking antidepressants. Darcy and I tried to convince her not to stop working, and that going back to the rest of her life, the same way she'd advised Bruce's friends to, would ultimately be the best thing for her. But the death part of her job in palliative care—which she'd always been so good at handling—now seemed too much for her. When I asked her what was wrong, she'd say, "I have a dead son." She was only half-joking.

The aftermath of Bruce's death was difficult for everyone.

For Anne and me, we reflected long and hard about what those final few years had been like for him, first and foremost. When someone with a substance-use disorder struggles in recovery, as Bruce had, they can feel such a sense of guilt and shame and helplessness. Which in turn can lead to hopelessness and relapsing even harder: *Fuck it, I don't care anymore and I'm done even trying.* The illness is also progressive, meaning it can intensify with every relapse.

To look at it from the outside, Bruce had an ideal support network. He had a loving family, financial support, and access to some of the best treatment available in this country. And he still couldn't do it. As if the addiction itself wasn't hard enough, addicts also have to deal with the intense societal stigma, and shame, that comes with it.

Most Canadians understand, by now, that addiction is a disease. And yet individual addicts are still blamed for it, as if it was simply a matter of making better life choices. But who grows up dreaming of being a drug addict? Who would *choose* to live a life full of such pain and desperation? Nobody. Bruce certainly didn't. But he fell victim to it anyway.

No matter how many other people were tied up in his drug-using behaviour, Anne and I never blamed anybody. The fact is that nobody ever held Bruce down and jammed drugs down his throat. We weren't even upset with Simon House and its punitive policy, which was the equivalent of saying, "You *should* be ashamed of yourself. Now go out there and do what you're going to do"—which is exactly what he did. Simon House did an incredible amount of good for Bruce during his two stays there, and we all knew the rules when he moved in. (Incidentally, Simon House has changed that policy in recent years, and the mandatory one-year ban is no longer in effect.)

And we tried not to blame ourselves, either. We often thought of how we had kept sending Bruce money or bailing him out of difficult situations—had we actually helped him? Wouldn't it have been better to force him to figure things out on his own from the start? In the end, we didn't think so. After Bruce died, Anne used to tell people, "We don't feel guilty about 'enabling' Bruce because it gave us two or three more years with him that we wouldn't have had otherwise." Obviously we would never tell someone else what they should do, should they find themselves in similar circumstances.

Anne and I lost a lot of sleep over the death of our firstborn child.

But not one minute of that was spent worrying about *coulda, woulda, shoulda*. We knew we'd tried everything we possibly could to help Bruce, and we were grateful for every extra moment that we got to spend with him as a result.

On that initial flight out to Calgary, on our way to get Bruce's body, Anne and I decided to write his obituary together. It was important to us to say what had really happened, and not shy away from the harsh reality of what he'd gone through. Even before he died, whenever people asked how Bruce was doing, Anne would look them in the eye and say, "He's struggling with addiction, but we're doing everything we can to help him."

I didn't hide it, either. All of my colleagues at work knew about Bruce's problem. Addiction is a nasty, ugly disease, no doubt about it. But it affects so many people in this country, many of whom suffer in silence. Anne and I made a point of talking about it, because we didn't see any shame in what had happened to our son.

Sadness, yes. But not shame.

So when it came to the obituary, we decided we weren't going to hide there, either. Which is why the first line reads, "Tragically, on March 28, 2011, Bruce Oake lost his battle with addiction at the tender age of 25."

Really, it was that philosophy of openness and honesty that became the genesis of the project that would consume Anne's and my lives for the next ten years.

Nine

The Beginning

Anne and I knew early on that we wanted to do something to commemorate Bruce's life. But it took time to figure out what that might look like.

Grief takes different forms for everybody. It's not uniform. Losing our child had devastated Anne and me, and there were many days when we weren't up for doing much of anything. But eventually we came to realize that we wanted to give voice to our grief—to take what had happened to us and use it to try to make a difference. Because as tragic as his death had been, the truth was that Bruce's story wasn't one in a million. In 2011 alone, more than 36,000 people in North America died from a drug overdose. It was a staggering statistic (and it's only grown worse since). If our story had the possibility of putting even the slightest dent in those numbers, shouldn't we try?

The first idea came from a close family friend named Ross Ruth-erford, who I'd worked with at CBC for many years. He is a big guy with an even bigger personality, and always seems to have a thousand ideas bubbling up in his mind. One day he suggested to us, "Why don't you set up a fund in Bruce's name at the Winnipeg Founda-tion?"

The Winnipeg Foundation is a charity and community founda-tion that helps people raise money and establish grants for a variety of causes. Every city has a similar organization, but the Winnipeg Foun-dation is the oldest such group in Canada, and they facilitate a lot of great work, including the Canadian Museum for Human Rights, which received the foundation's largest-ever grant in 2003.

With Ross's encouragement, Anne and I set up the Bruce Oake Fund, which had two goals. The first, more modest one was rais-ing money in order to pay for treatment for addicts who otherwise couldn't afford it—because we knew from our experience with Bruce that finances were the single largest barrier to sobriety. That alone could make a real difference. But our real dream, which Anne and I discussed at length but had no real idea how to pull off, was some-thing much more ambitious: opening a nonprofit treatment centre here in Winnipeg.

There were existing options for treatment within the city, of course. But the need already outpaced the number of beds available, and the opioid crisis was only getting worse. One study found that, by 2010, more than 5 percent of Canadians were using prescription opioids for nonmedical purposes.

Plus, Anne and I had really come to respect and appreciate the philosophy of Simon House, and we wanted to establish a facility in

Manitoba that had a similar approach. That meant providing treatment at no cost (with the complex fundraising and logistical hoops that came with it). And, just as importantly, it meant offering a continuum of care: where clients could stay as long as they needed to and retained access to important resources even after they left. Bruce's eleven months at Simon House were by far the best year of his addicted life. We wanted to see if we could find a way to offer that same experience to others in need.

But how to actually do it? We had no idea. The first step in that direction happened almost by accident. A few months after Bruce died, our godson Bret was working as manager of one of the JOEY restaurants here in Winnipeg, and he got to talking with one of his regular customers. This guy's name was Todd Lovallo, and in addition to being the co-owner of a company called Vertuity Mortgage, he was starting up a charity golf tournament that August. The two of them got talking, and Bruce's story came up. Todd might look like kind of a tough guy, but beneath the surface he's very caring and compassionate. By the end of the conversation, he had agreed to donate part of the tournament's funds to this long-range—some might say far-fetched—project of ours.

To show our gratitude, I spoke to the group of golfers at that initial tournament, and convinced my colleague Kelly Hrudey to fly in and say a few words, too. This wasn't a fully prepared speech or anything, but when I started talking about Bruce, you could've heard a pin drop in the room. Something in his story really captured their attention. It was inspiring. And the total amount of money raised ended up being around $12,000, which was an incredible amount of money to us. (It also marked the beginning of a great partnership, as we've been lucky enough to receive the full proceeds of that tournament every year since, which has become a staple of our fundraising efforts.) That weekend was the first time Anne and I thought this crazy idea of ours might actually work.

In April 2012, just a year after Bruce's death, we had our first chance to see how the idea would be received on a national scale when Bruce Dowbiggin wrote an article about Bruce for the *Globe and Mail*. In it, he told the whole story of Bruce's struggles with addiction, and mentioned that Anne and I wanted to raise "awareness and money for an as-yet-unnamed addiction facility in Winnipeg." This was true, though in reality we had no idea how we might actually build such a facility. It didn't matter: once the story was distributed to newsstands across the country, donations started to roll in.

Because the idea was still in its early stages, every donation we received went through the Winnipeg Foundation, who would then issue tax receipts in the donor's name. Anne and I also received personal cheques sent directly to our home, and these we also forwarded to the Winnipeg Foundation. The amounts really varied. In addition to the golf tournament fundraiser, there was an assistant manager at JOEY named Sean Lough, who'd made some money in the stock market, and one day he handed us a personal cheque for $10,000. Around the same time, a good friend of mine named Don Baizley passed away, and his family donated $10,000 to us as well. Pretty soon we'd accumulated more than $50,000.

In 2014, we took the next step, and became a registered charity called the Bruce Oake Memorial Foundation. This meant branching away from the Winnipeg Foundation, which allowed us to manage our own money and raise our profile in the community. It also meant we could issue our own tax receipts to donors, which Anne recognized as an opportunity. Every couple of weeks, she and her friends Brenda and Kathy would sit at our kitchen table and prepare these receipts, along with a handwritten note from Anne thanking each donor by name. It was a special touch that many people appreciated, and Anne continued doing it even when there were so many donations her hand would cramp up.

Around that time we also formed our first Board of Directors. Anne and I didn't have any experience in this realm, so we mostly recruited family and friends who we thought could help push the project forward. These included Ross Rutherford, who had encouraged us to set up the initial fund with the Winnipeg Foundation; Todd Lovallo from the golf tournament; Susan Millican, a longtime friend from the CBC who was also the Winnipeg Foundation's outgoing chairperson; Drew Cringen, who owned a local ad agency; and a vice president at the accounting firm MNP named Brett Franklin. I met Brett at the very first golf tournament, and thanks to his presence on the board, MNP prepared five different business plans for us over the years, each of which was revised constantly. I didn't realize just how much of a favour this was until I met someone else who'd paid full freight for one MNP business plan—to the tune of five figures!

In those early years, pretty much everything we did happened on a small scale and by the seat of our pants. Once we'd become a registered charity, Anne also went back and added up everything we'd received to that point in grassroots donations, which refers to one-time, smaller amounts like $25, $50, or $100. Somehow, it added up to around $80,000. That's an awful lot of $50 bills. But to us, it was a sign that we were getting into the public consciousness, and that people were getting behind the project. We saw those donations as representing the will of the community. And it was clear the community was voting solidly in favour of a recovery centre.

Now that money was starting to come in, the board decided to start putting it to use. The first thing we did was hire a consultant named Leslie Lindberg to write a needs study for us, which is a document that lays out the need for whatever you're trying to get done—in our case, a not-for-profit recovery centre. As part of her research, Leslie went to Calgary to spend time at Simon House and learn more about how they operated. While she was there, however, Leslie heard about another treatment centre in the city called Fresh Start. When she came back to Winnipeg, she told us Fresh Start was what we should really be shooting for. It had a similar philosophy to Simon House, but Fresh Start's facility is what really bowled Leslie over. The building was beautiful and warm, she told us—the kind of place you'd want to live permanently, if you could. That sure got our attention.

But if we were ever going to raise enough money to put shovels in the ground for an actual building, we needed to start moving up to where the really big sums are found. The board hired two fundraising consultants also helped us arrange some initial meetings with people who might be sympathetic to our cause. There was value in all of it, but we still weren't getting very far.

The strategies that seemed to work best for us were when we could tell people Bruce's story on a personal level. I was at the gym one day in 2015 when I ran into Jeff Thompson, who at the time was the president of the Winnipeg chapter of the Young Presidents' Organization, a collective of executives from around the world. I told him what we were working on, and he invited Anne and me to come speak to his group. So we put together a forty-minute presentation about Bruce's life, which included several video clips to help show the audience what kind of person Bruce was. Our only condition was that it had to be honest. We didn't leave anything out—from the assault in the stash house to being found in the bathroom stall with the needle in his arm. But we also showed Bruce's sense of humour, and his love of boxing and rap music. The presentation was meant to show people just how much potential he had, and how addiction had tragically taken that potential away. It wasn't difficult to prepare, because it was all true.

Before we gave that first presentation, I remember Anne being extremely nervous to speak in front of such a large crowd. Like a lot of people, she was calm and collected in her own world, but when it came to public speaking she tensed up. To get through it as pain-lessly as possible, she was adamant that we stick to the script we'd written—and she did. I, on the other hand, went up there and imme-diately started ad-libbing a bunch of extra details about Darcy, who was familiar to the crowd because of his work as a magician. This drove Anne nuts, because every time I went off script, she'd lose her place. She kept it under control while we were up there, but definitely made her displeasure known as soon as we stepped offstage.

We were hopeful that people would be sympathetic to Bruce's story, but even we weren't prepared for the type of response we got that evening. Once we finished, there were several people eager to tell us their own stories about family members who'd struggled or were currently struggling with addiction, and how they were trying to deal with it. It really underscored that this was a big problem—and it mo-tivated us to keep going, and to keep telling the story.

The next time we delivered the presentation was at a luncheon at a local Rotary Club, at the invitation of a good friend named Ted Foreman. Word had obviously travelled, because the place was jam-packed. Once again, the presentation ended with Anne and me telling the crowd about what we hoped to do, which was build a treatment centre in Bruce's name. And once again there was a line of people waiting for us afterwards, all of whom wanted to tell us the stories of their own encounters with addiction. The problem, we were learning ever more vividly, was even more widespread than we'd realized. It turned out you didn't have to shake any family tree too hard to get an alcoholic or an addict to fall out.

No matter what we tried, the big selling point was always our story—the story of Bruce's life and tragic death. That never changed, and it's still the case today. Having a personal story that people could relate to was always our most valuable tool.

On the grassroots level, we were doing extremely well. Word had made its way around Winnipeg about our project, thanks in part to our presentation and in part to media stories like the one in the *Globe*. Handwritten cheques appeared in our mailbox nearly every day, adding thousands of additional dollars to the fund. One Christmas I remember Anne opening envelope after envelope after envelope, until there was more than $50,000 spread out on our kitchen table.

But there was still a feeling that the project wasn't moving fast enough—and our board wasn't really sure why, or what to do about it. We held regular meetings, with agendas full of real topics of discussion, but we just weren't getting anywhere. Our needs study laid out the number of overdose deaths in Winnipeg, the amount of resources being spent on 911 calls related to drugs, and the lack of treatment beds for people looking to get sober. With those statistics in hand, we met with various contacts in both the local and provincial governments. But our inexperience was showing. We couldn't figure out how to build on our initial momentum, and several months later we'd find ourselves meeting with the same people all over again. Throughout our board discussions, there was one nagging question we never had an answer to: *how do we put this into action?*

It was frustrating at times, because to Anne and me, the need for what we wanted to build was blindingly obvious. Canada was in the middle of a national opioid crisis. People were dying by the thousands— and this was before fentanyl entered the picture a few years later and made everything ten times worse.

When we met with politicians during this time, I would ask them, "If you were an addict, and you woke up one morning and wanted to change your life, what would you do?" Within Winnipeg there was only one option for medical detox, but it was always full. Plus, even if that worked, detox is only the starting point. Then you need actual treatment. The only government-run treatment program was at the AFM, and they, too, usually had a huge waitlist. Meanwhile the private programs were out of reach for many people financially.

I told these politicians that the way things currently stood, we were leaving a generation of addicts out there to die. That wasn't hyperbole.

Then came the meth crisis, which showed the awful reality of drug addiction from another angle. Meth was another national problem, but Winnipeg was hit especially hard—in a private conversation, our local fire chief described the city as ground zero for this particular drug. There were news stories every day about meth-induced psychosis and crime. Meth is so cheap, and it can swallow you whole. A person could beg at a traffic light for an hour and earn enough to stay high for the rest of the day. It felt for a long time here that it was tearing a hole in the heart of the city. And I'm sure it was the same in other cities.

For Anne and me, we could only hope that these stories in the media would help raise awareness about the overall drug crisis we were facing as a society, and highlight the importance of a treatment centre like the one we wanted to build. Whenever we spoke in public, Anne and I tried to make the case that the only way out of this crisis was through treatment. That is the only way for addicts to get their lives back, and once again become functioning members of society. It was an outcome everyone should be cheering for, and I think most people recognized that.

While our wheels were spinning in terms of top-tier donations, we kept at our grassroots efforts. Donations were still coming in, largely from within Manitoba. This made sense, considering that's how we positioned our pitch, and where the treatment centre would ultimately be located. But we also received support from other parts of the country. The Thorpe Recovery Centre in Lloydminster, Saskatchewan, for example, invited Anne and me to come out and give our presentation, and gave us a cheque for $10,000 when we got there. Rogers Sportsnet also agreed to donate national airtime for two PSAs we created, and we could tell whenever the ads ran because money would inevitably start flowing in. It was mostly smaller amounts, but even a handful of $100 donations adds up. We were grateful for everyone who donated anything at all to the cause.

The first sign that things were about to change for us was when I got a phone call from Todd Lovallo, organizer of the golf charity tournament. He said to me, "There's a woman about to drive through Winnipeg who works for Fresh Start. I think you should go meet her."

The woman's name was Lisa Simone, and at the time she was Fresh Start's director of public relations. Todd knew her because she happened to be the cousin of one of his business partners, which is how he learned that Lisa was in the process of moving from Calgary to Niagara Falls, where she was planning to continue working for Fresh Start remotely.

I was willing to meet with anyone, so I reached out to Lisa, and we met up at a Tim Hortons about a half-mile from our house. In retrospect, this innocuous-seeming meeting was a major turning point for us. Lisa and I ended up talking for probably two hours. She had a compelling story—like everyone at Fresh Start, Lisa was in recovery herself, and had also lost her husband to an overdose—and she was extremely knowledgeable about Fresh Start's philosophy and operations. She was also generous, and in addition to offering to introduce me to several of her colleagues, she handed me a thumb drive containing all of Fresh Start's financial statements from the past few years.

What am I going to do with this? I thought. *I can hardly balance my own chequebook!*

"You should think about building a place like Fresh Start here," Lisa told me. "If you do, we'll do everything we can to help you."

From there, we struck up a relationship with Fresh Start, and they guided us through the whole process, just as Lisa promised. It was a stroke of absolute good luck on our part, and I can't thank them enough.

When telling the story of how the Bruce Oake Recovery Centre came into existence, there are two people we met who deserve special credit for all they did for us. One is Lisa Simone. The other one, who we met shortly afterwards, and who ended up changing everything for us, is Marni Larkin.

Four Years, Nine Votes,
Two Politicians, and
One Boarded-Up Arena

In November 2016, I was asked by Bob Kozminski, one of our board members and a well-known businessman, to emcee an annual event called the Duff Roblin Dinner. Held at the Fort Garry Hotel, this is a high-profile event that honours people from around Manitoba for their citizenship and community work. In return, Bob told me he could probably arrange a meeting for us with the deputy premier, whom he also knew. At that time, Manitoba was a few years into the first Brian Pallister majority government, and we knew that if we were ever going to get our project off the ground, we would need their support.

So of course I said okay.

It was an interesting enough evening, but the most memorable part for me was the woman who had organized it. Her name was Marni Larkin, and I could tell right away she was a pit bull: determined and extremely loyal. She owned an event company called Boom Done Next along with her colleague, Joe Leuzzi, and the name was apt. She was a person who got shit done, quickly and efficiently. Marni and I got to talking, and when I told her about our idea for the treatment centre, she told me she might be able to help.

She said, "Come see me at my office tomorrow."

I did, and from that point onwards I was hanging over her desk at least once a week asking for advice and picking up tips.

True to her word, Marni got to work for us right away. She'd done lots of work for other organizations in the past, and what really piqued my interest was that she knew how government worked at both the civic and provincial level. Following the dinner, we did get that promised meeting from Bob with Deputy Premier Heather Stefanson, and while she gave us a warm reception and seemed to understand the problem, nothing ultimately came of it. Marni, on the other hand, organized a separate meeting for us with the City of Winnipeg that she thought could really get the ball rolling and ask the mayor directly for a surplus building.

She'd also advised us to invite Stacey Petersen, then the executive director of Fresh Start in Calgary, for both meetings, because she thought his expertise would increase our odds of success at the meeting with the city. Anne and I agreed.

We knew Stacey through my chance meeting with Lisa Simone, and from there, I'd had a number of phone calls with him. Anne and I had also flown out and seen Fresh Start in person. Their main piece of advice to us was: "Build the kind of place where you'd want to live."

It was certainly advice they'd followed in their own facility—the first time I saw it, I was sure I was in the wrong place, and that I'd accidentally sent the taxi to some kind of high-end modern condo instead.

Stacey and I had a good relationship, and he and his staff, including director of operations Bruce Holstead, were instrumental in guiding us through our own process from afar.

The two of us met with both Mayor Brian Bowman and his chief of staff, Jason Fuith, on December 5, 2016. Right away, this meeting felt different from similar ones we'd attended in the past. Health is technically a provincial jurisdiction, but it was the cities that were seeing the dramatic results of the drug crisis up close and personal. Meth was raging in Winnipeg, and fentanyl was on the rise. There were daily news stories documenting the pain and suffering. It was impossible to escape, and everyone was searching for solutions.

We took Marni's advice and asked the city for a surplus building—which basically meant a city-owned property that wasn't currently being used for anything—in order to give our project a head start towards completion. It was a big ask, and one that we hadn't even thought of making until Marni suggested it. But to my surprise, the mayor took our request seriously. And Marni was also right to have Stacey there, because he could speak eloquently about the philosophy of the centre we wanted to build. (It also helped our cause because Stacey had done a bunch of work for Calgary mayor Naheed Nenshi, who was an esteemed professional colleague of Bowman's.) Stacey gave our pitch added credibility, whereas I was just some blabbermouth pseudo-celebrity who could be easily ignored.

At the end of the meeting, Fuith thanked us for coming in and told us, "I'll get back to you before Christmas."

And, sure enough, he did. This time, he came to us with a list of potential surplus properties—one of which was the old Vimy Arena in a West End neighbourhood called Crestview.

The Vimy Arena was built back in 1972, and had been a longtime staple of the surrounding community of St. James. But there were issues with it from the beginning, from the building materials used to the size of the dressing rooms. Over time the arena had become run-down, and eventually the city decided to close it in 2015, and it had sat, boarded up, ever since. At some point there had been discussions on renovating the rink, but it had been deemed not worth the cost of bringing it up to code. Instead, the abandoned building had become a magnet for sketchy behaviour and crime, especially at night. If you wanted to buy or use drugs in that neighbourhood back then, you went to Vimy. It wasn't uncommon for the police to be called there. And because Vimy wasn't ever going to reopen, the city had deemed it a surplus property.

When we saw Vimy on the list, our first thought was, *What on earth are we going to do with an old hockey rink?* But Anne and I decided to drive out and see it, which we did in early 2017, along with a few of our board members and three staff from MMP Architects, who we were working with us on the design of the future treatment centre. As we toured the property, I quickly realized it as the perfect site. We knew we'd never find a better site than this one.

For one thing, Vimy was in a residential area, but it didn't border anyone's house directly—in other words, you wouldn't be looking over the fence into someone else's backyard. Second, it was on a bus route, which meant it was accessible to people who didn't own a car. Third, and maybe most important, it overlooked both beautiful

Sturgeon Creek and the serene trail system that wove through it. *This,* I thought, *is a place where a person could get better.*

As for the existing building, it didn't take long for our architects to agree with the city's assessment. It couldn't be saved. The whole thing would need to come down, after which they could construct a beautiful new building to replace it. Anne and I were sold just as quickly. In fact, we didn't even go look at any other options on the list, because we agreed there could be no better place. The location was just perfect. Sure, it would require a little more work than lightly renovating a building that was already pretty much good to go, which had been our initial idea. But it was clear there was an opportunity here to replace the boarded-up, graffiti-covered crime magnet with a state-of-the-art structure. We were going to take a place where you would go to score, and turn it into a place of hope. It was perfect.

At the same time, we understood that the Vimy Arena had been a beloved gathering place for residents of the area. There was a lot of history in that building. Plenty of people had fond memories of their kids playing there, or learning to skate there themselves, and that nostalgia made it difficult for some of them to accept that the building was not just past its prime, but never to reopen.

With a project like ours, we were prepared for some backlash. But what happened to us next was more than anyone could have expected.

In the meantime, however, we kept on raising money and awareness for our cause. The United Firefighters of Winnipeg agreed to make the Bruce Oake Memorial Foundation the beneficiary for two of their galas, which added up to around $30,000 in total. Anne also gave a talk to the Manitoba Nurses Union, which led to another generous $30,000 donation. And that March, I was chosen as the honouree at the Pan Am Clinic's annual Fire & Ice Gala—I guess because they finally ran out of real guests. I didn't really want to attend, because the idea of sitting on a stage while a bunch of people applaud and say nice things about me makes me uncomfortable. But Darcy made a pretty convincing argument: I believe his exact words were, "Cut the bullshit, Scotty, you've got to do this." It's one of the biggest dinners in Winnipeg, and I realized it was another opportunity for us to really get into the public consciousness. So I did it, and that night probably brought in another $50,000 worth of donations.

At around the same time, Darcy decided to put on four benefit shows at the Burton Cummings Theatre in Winnipeg. Thanks to his appearances on shows like *Britain's Got Talent*, he was well known as a world-class illusionist, and all four shows sold out. The best trick of all, however, was performed ahead of time by Ross Rutherford, our board member, who was never afraid to ask people for something if he thought it was worthwhile. So he cold-called Bonnie and John Buhler, a very wealthy philanthropic family whose names are attached to a lot of things in Winnipeg. The Buhlers knew Ross, and they actually knew our family, too, because Darcy had been in the Winnipeg Magic Club with one of their grandsons.

Ross told them the Bruce Oake Recovery Centre was about to get going. Would they consider making a donation?

The thing to know about the Buhlers is that they get these kinds of calls all the time, about all kinds of crazy ideas and projects. But

Old Vimy Arena.

I think they recognized the severity of the opioid crisis, and Ross made a convincing pitch. By the end of the phone call, they'd agreed to match whatever amount Darcy raised at his shows. This worked out to around $50,000 apiece, or $200,000 in total, which meant our bank account was suddenly nearly half a million dollars richer. I remember looking at the balance shortly afterwards and saying to Anne, "Hey, we might be able to get this thing done after all!"

Once we'd settled on the Vimy site as our preferred location, we had to then go through a complicated process by which the surplus property would be leased to us for a nominal fee—in our case, $1 per year for ninety-nine years. Because an addiction treatment centre falls under the category of health, which is a provincial jurisdiction, the province needed to be involved as well. The way it worked, the province needed to officially request and receive the building from the city, at which point they could lease it to the Bruce Oake Memorial Foundation.

It was a legitimate process, albeit a little-known one, but as soon as word got out about what was happening, the city started taking fire. The most common complaint was that we shouldn't have simply been handed the building; it should instead have gone out to a request for proposals (or RFP), so that other interested groups could have had a chance to bid on it. I understood that line of thinking, but disagreed with it. The city gave us the building because they wanted us to have it. The building would cost too much money to bring back up to code, no matter who was going to take over the land. This wasn't a matter of squeezing the most possible money out of the site. The mayor simply recognized a widespread social problem and wanted to help with a solution. He was trying to cut through the red tape that otherwise

would've held us back for a long time, and I appreciated his leadership in this situation.

We were fortunate that both the city and the province were sup-
portive of our project, but there is a natural and unfortunate tendency
in government to offload responsibility whenever possible. In order
to officially receive the land where the Vimy Arena stood, we needed
a letter of support from the provincial minister of health, stating that
they were requesting the city's help in establishing a treatment centre, which I would then give to the city. They'd agreed to provide
this letter, but actually acquiring it proved far more difficult. There
were several weeks where I'd be trying to focus on preparing for that
weekend's *Hockey Night in Canada* telecast, but having to make one
last phone call to the government as the doors of the plane closed for
takeoff. Finally the letter arrived, and from there it was over to the
mayor's office, where the process continued.

Throughout this process, Anne, Darcy, and I never lost sight of
Bruce, and we always took time to remember him on his birthday, as
well as the day of his death. The three of us made a point of getting
together—not to have a showy ceremony or anything, but just to be
near one another and spend time as a family. Inevitably, though, the
stories would start to come: Bruce's struggles to learn how to ride a
bike, and his success in the boxing ring. Anne also kept a CD of his
raps, which she would play all the time in her car while driving. The
lyrics were far more graphic than anything she normally listened to,
but being able to hear her son's voice again outweighed anything he
might have been rapping about.

We kept speaking and raising money during the summer, while
City Council was prorogued, and that fall it all got up and running

again. In October, I went with Russell Krepart, one of MMP's senior architects (and later one of its owner-principals), to meet with the executive policy committee, which is sort of like the mayor's cabinet. I appreciated working with MMP, because they sent representatives to all of our meetings with the city and helped answer a lot of the technical questions I didn't know anything about.

After this particular meeting was over, we got word that the area councillor, a man named Shawn Dobson, was not happy with us. He wasn't part of the executive policy committee, but he felt that he'd been frozen out of the process, and as a result was furious that the city was considering giving us this property—within his riding—without him knowing about it. We understood his anger, and met with him privately to ask that he hold off on going public about his position until he'd had a chance to see the good work that Fresh Start was doing in Calgary. But Dobson didn't care. He held a press conference the next afternoon denouncing the project, and from that day on we had a target on our backs.

Dobson felt, for whatever reason, that a recovery centre had no place in his riding. He tried to argue that recovery centres should only be put in rural or industrial areas—where he got such an idea, I have no clue. He also drew into the fray another group in the city called Equal Opportunities West, which provided employment for mentally handicapped adults. They happened to also be looking for a new facility, and Dobson decided to say publicly that *they* should be given the Vimy Arena site, not us.

Essentially, he was pitting one nonprofit group against another, which was unfair to both of us. Not to mention that our needs were completely different. We wanted to build a brand-new, multimillion-dollar facility, and they didn't. I don't know how that building could have ever been repurposed in a way that would have suited Equal Opportunities. It didn't really make sense. But Dobson was out to sink us, full stop.

From that point onwards, Anne and I suddenly had to spend a lot of our time defending ourselves, and the project, in the local media. Suffice to say, this wasn't what we'd signed up for. It felt like we were living that old saying, where no good deed goes unpunished. But it was obviously a juicy story for TV, radio, and print reporters. And, really, we weren't even upset with most of the coverage. We understood that people in the area had concerns about building a treatment centre. You have to expect pushback for a project like ours, especially in a residential area. I believed that when questions and concerns arose, it was our responsibility to run an education campaign—which we did. Anne and I did our best to channel Bruce's dogged determination and to keep going, even when it felt like the battle would never end.

We had countless email exchanges with individual residents who'd contacted us to tell us they were dead set against the centre. I spent hours at my keyboard, trying to win people over, and my success rate was higher than you might think. People don't know what they don't know, and I did my best to explain how a treatment centre works—it's fundamentally different, for instance, than a safe-injection site—and how we were going to clean up this problem building and put something new and helpful in its place.

I remember one exchange where the guy came in particularly hot, and by the end of our conversation he was asking how he could make a small donation. Another woman was completely against the project until her daughter got involved, and explained to her how many people she personally knew who had struggled with drugs. Darcy did his part, too, making a video that cleared up misconceptions and explained what the project was really all about.

We also installed a second phone line at our home, dedicated to the Bruce Oake Memorial Foundation. The number was public, and you would not believe some of the abusive, vitriolic messages we received there, too. People who didn't want drug addicts ruining their neighbourhood, or people who just wanted to call Anne and me idiots. Some of these messages were so extreme, Anne would play them out loud to her friends just to prove she wasn't exaggerating.

As this public debate raged on, Steven Fletcher showed up and like Dobson, Fletcher did everything he could possibly think of to sink us. He was a politician who used to be a federal MP in Stephen Harper's cabinet, and once his federal career was over, he ran provincially and won as the MLA in the riding that included St. James and the Vimy Arena. But he'd been booted out of the Conservative caucus and so was running again as an independent in the upcoming provincial election. He was clearly looking for an issue that he could ride to electoral victory, and when he saw this red-hot topic happening in his riding, he jumped on it.

At the same time, Dobson started organizing public meetings—again, with no facts behind them—with the goal of whipping his constituents into a lather. One of these took place at the Assiniboine Memorial Curling Club, which was located directly next door to Vimy. Both he and Fletcher kept repeating the same talking points, chief among them this idea that a treatment centre should only be located in a rural or industrial area. It wasn't just incorrect: it was cold-hearted. In that part of St. James, there is a combination of young people buying their first homes and elderly folks who've lived there for decades. If you're a senior citizen, and a former federal cabinet minister comes along and tells you that this scary project is going to tank your property values, you're probably going to believe them. Many people in that age bracket just didn't understand how modern drug culture worked. When they were young, the only thing society did with drug users was throw them in jail. There was no conception of the role of a recovery centre, and Fletcher was playing on that ignorance in order to fan the flames of fear.

I wanted so badly to respond and try to set things straight, but Marni wouldn't let me. She told me to stay above the fray. And so I did. We corrected Fletcher and Dobson about Fresh Start's location multiple times—yes, it technically bordered a light industrial area on one side, but the critical piece was that it was within walking distance of more than one neighbourhood, and as a result the residents were part of the surrounding community. They were good neighbours. The best shot residents have at being successful in recovery is when they feel they are included in a community. Being isolated and stigmatized is a bad combination, which is why rural and industrial areas went so strongly against our philosophy. But Fletcher and Dobson were relentless, and in beating this rural/industrial idea to death, many in the area were willing to believe them.

Fletcher did actually go to Fresh Start in person. He flew out to Calgary with two aides and banged on the front door with no advance warning. Luckily, Bruce Holstead happened to be there, and he gave them a tour of the place. The residents were in good spirits that day, and Fletcher was welcomed with open arms—in fact, one of the guys came up to him and said, "Oh, are you new? You'll love it here!"

One of Fletcher's aides was so impressed by what she saw that at one point she started crying. But then, when it was over, Fletcher went out front and made a video for his supporters repeating the same old talking points. It was like he hadn't heard a single word anyone had said.

I only found out about this visit when I got a phone call one afternoon from the *Winnipeg Free Press*, asking me for a response to his latest video. It was so disheartening. Pushback is part of the process, and it was our job to get through to people. But I believe Fletcher was being deliberately disingenuous, and was more focused on his own political livelihood than the well-being of his constituents. He kept referring to "the good people of St. James," but really I believe he was only trying to help himself. In the process, he made our job far more difficult than it otherwise needed to be.

Dobson was no better. The thing he kept telling us was, "If my residents don't want it, I don't want it."

I asked him, "Why wouldn't you consider being a leader on this issue? Why not let your constituents know how great of a need there is here?"

But he wasn't interested—despite the fact, by the way, that some of the people who would become participants of the recovery centre were *also* his constituents. According to one person I spoke with, St. James had more recovery groups per capita than anywhere else in Winnipeg. There were drug busts happening in a couple of places not far from the Vimy Arena. Police were in the area on a regular basis. We weren't just offering to build something that would improve the neighbourhood: our recovery centre was going to directly help save the lives of the some of the same people whose interests Dobson claimed to represent. But we simply could not get through to him.

By November, the treatment centre had become such a hot-button issue that there was all kinds of new misinformation being spread around. People were arguing that, for instance, we were actually building a *for-profit* centre that would secretly make us a whole bunch of money. The idea that we would try to profit off the death of our son was repugnant, and untrue across the board.

When Marni found out about these accusations, she called me and said, "Okay, we need to get the truth out there. What do you think of an information session? We can have it at the MMP office, and we can invite all of the councillors and city managers to set the record straight." Well, in Marni's world, *What do you think about* is code for *This is what we're going to do.* Plus, Anne and I thought it was a great idea. So that's what we did.

At that meeting, we were finally able to convince Dobson that we were a registered charity, and that every penny we raised was going to go into the running of the centre. He told us that was all well and good, but he still didn't support it.

After that, we decided it was time to make our case directly to the public. We held our first public information session at the Sturgeon Heights Community Club on December 5, 2017, and it quickly turned nasty. We brought in Stacey and Bruce from Fresh Start to describe how their centre operated, but most of the residents who showed up were already outraged, based on what they'd heard ahead of time from Fletcher and Dobson. The venue held around three hundred people, and it was jammed full. Emotions were running high across the board.

Ultimately, much of the anger we encountered was based on a misunderstanding. Once we actually heard the complaints that people had, we realized they had no idea what the Bruce Oake Recovery Centre was intended to do, or how it would work. Many people who were upset, for instance, didn't seem to know the basic difference between active addiction and recovery—and the gap between these two things is profound. Active addiction means you're currently using drugs, and the rest of your day is spent in the single-minded pursuit of getting more. Whereas recovery means not just being sober, but also actively working on your sobriety. Our treatment centre wasn't going to result in a pile of used needles in the street. It would be a gathering place for people who have admitted they need help with their addictions, and who are dedicated to making changes in their lives. We tried to tell those who objected to the project that people coming to the Bruce Oake Recovery Centre were going to be focused on one thing: their sobriety.

There were positive stories in the anger, too. One of them is that whenever Dobson and Fletcher went public against us, other people rallied to our defence. For example, Jonathan Parker, a young guy who lived in Crestview and struggled with addiction, became a warrior for us. Addiction had cost him his very promising hockey career, and he'd been in recovery for a number of years. When he learned about our project, he came to our aid and spoke on our behalf in public. He had no other vested interest in the issue aside from his belief that this was something that was needed. Sobriety had made Jonathan a better brother and son, and he wanted people to have the same shot at recovery that he'd had.

Then there was Carol Janke, a minister who lived within sight of the Vimy Arena. She was a respected member of the community, and she also became an advocate for the project. Reverend Janke reminded everyone how much sketchy behaviour was currently happening at the shuttered building, and described in harrowing detail the night that a woman died there in the freezing cold. Human stories like these, I believe, helped get our point across even more effectively than the statistics could.

The truth was, we couldn't really say all that much before we officially had the property, because it would have been presumptuous. We were in the middle of a lengthy, complex bureaucratic process, and there were no guarantees that we'd even make it to the finish line. In order to receive the land from the city, we had to win a vote at four different levels of government: a community committee, the property and development committee, the executive policy committee, and, finally, City Council. If we could pass all four votes, the city could then put the surplus property into a provincial inventory, which then allowed the province to lease it to us at the nominal fee of $1 per year.

There was a lot of work to be done to even *get* to that first vote, which happened on January 8, 2018. And at every one of the votes, members of the public were invited to show up and speak, either for or against the proposed project.

Once again, Fletcher and Dobson did their best to get people to come out and speak against it. Sometimes Anne and I would show up and see twenty or thirty names listed on the speaker list. It really was frustrating at times that these residents would rather have kept a dilapidated building than turn it into something positive. But at the same time, I understood how they'd reached that place, based on the misinformation they'd been given. We'd done our best to educate people, and now it came down to the city.

We managed to win that first vote, and then the next one, and then the one after that.

Finally, Council was set to have the final vote on January 25. When the results were counted, it was 11–3 in favour of giving us the land—which is actually a lot narrower than it looks. We needed to win by eight votes in order for it to count, and we only barely got there. A couple of sympathetic councillors were away that day, and I remember running around at the last minute, trying to lobby for extra votes while the councillors were on their lunch break.

It looked like the vote was going to come down to one councillor in particular. I was so out of my element, it was a joke. Anne and I never figured out the subtle language of politics: we always just spoke from the heart.

"We lost our son," I told the councillor again. "We don't want it to happen to anyone else—but it is, right now, all around Winnipeg. This is our chance to do something about it."

In the end, it worked. We got the votes. Which meant we officially had the land.

This was not happy news for one of the groups organized against us. They were called the Friends of Sturgeon Creek, and they were against the recovery centre because they wanted to protect the green space around the nearby creek. The group was well organized, and we took their concern seriously. We'd argued that, should our proposal go ahead, the area would actually be *increasing* its amount of green space, because the treatment centre's footprint would be smaller than the arena's had been. We also made a promise that, once the centre was built, we would never expand towards the creek. Once the Council vote was finalized, a leader from the Friends of Sturgeon Creek came over and asked us to always be good stewards of the land. I assured them we would be.

Now that we had the property, the real work began. The next step was to get it rezoned, from recreational to residential mixed use. We had to get this done before we could apply for any of our development and construction permits, and it was, again, an exhausting process that dragged on through the summer.

As part of the rezoning process, we had to hold a series of four public information sessions, which were run by our architects at MMP. (Anne and I had been advised not to be there in person, because of how heated things had become at the previous session at the Sturgeon Heights Community Club.) The first two were held on August 14, and, once again, they were both raucous. People were yelling and holding up signs and placards.

Watching remotely, however, the thing I remember most about that day were Rodell and Jen Bautista, who had lost their son Gabriel just a few weeks earlier. He died from suicide, but before that had struggled with addiction for a long time. After hearing about their tragedy, I'd reached out to try to provide some small amount of sympathy for what they'd gone through. When I called Rodell, however, he said, "We're coming to the sessions." And they did—Rodell, Jen, and their four other children. This family was absolutely fearless, and they took on all comers. For as loudly as the opponents of the project wanted to shout the whole thing down, they got it back from the Bautistas, and then some. We were so grateful to have them in our corner.

The next two sessions were held on September 25, and had a somewhat different tone. The clearer-thinking people in the area focused on the fact that this process meant they were going to lose a rec centre. Technically, Vimy Arena was already done for, and had been for a long time. But it was a real loss nonetheless, and we wanted to be respectful of what it had meant to the neighbourhood for all those years.

So we instructed our architects to change the plans to include a public entrance to the new gym, including separate change rooms, so that neighbours could also book the gym for their own use. This was a small step on our end, but a meaningful one, and we were happy to do it. I believe it strengthened our relationship with the surrounding community and showed residents that there was nothing to fear from us. The men at Bruce Oake were going to be good neighbours, and this was another way to prove it.

My catchphrase at the time became, "If all criminals were sentenced to having to get a civic property rezoned, there would be no more crime." But our architects were detailed and diligent, and we slowly made our way through the whole process.

By November, it was back to City Hall to go through the whole voting process again, starting with the community committee, continuing to property and development and the executive policy committee, and then a final vote at Council. That made eight votes in total, which someone joked to me was surely a civic record for a single project.

The vocal opposition continued, much of which was still

disheartening in how much misinformation it contained. Leading up to the final vote at City Council, a group of people showed up for a last-gasp attempt to stop the property being rezoned—and the abject ignorance on display was stunning. One woman didn't like the idea of the public use of the gymnasium, and said in protest, "Who's going to clean the basketballs after the addicts use them?" Someone else insisted that taking drugs was a choice. As this was happening, Anne was sitting beside me, whispering, "Don't say anything. Don't groan. Don't make a face." At one point I couldn't take it anymore, and put my head in my hands. "Sit up," Anne said right away. "You have to look professional." She was right.

Dobson and Fletcher, too, refused to give up on the issue. They fought us right to the bitter end. As a provincial politician, Fletcher wasn't officially involved in any of these votes with the city, but he did attend them in person and sit up in the gallery. Dobson, meanwhile, was down on the floor, and it looked like he had Fletcher in his ear the whole time because there were times Dobson was reading out a message, then stopped mid-sentence and looked up at Fletcher, as if his teleprompter had run out of text.

In those final months, Fletcher partnered with an owner of a for-profit treatment centre located outside the city, and tried to make a deal with him, supposedly on our behalf. He got them to agree to give us a small piece of their property, in exchange for us giving up on redeveloping the Vimy site. But it was a nonstarter on our end, since placing our centre way out in a rural area went against everything we stood for—a fact that Fletcher well knew.

As Fletcher tried to frame it, however, this was a win-win solution that would solve everything, and he would come out of it looking like the hero. But before the initial press conference announcing this idea, the representative from the for-profit centre faced some pushback and showed up having already changed his tune—now, he claimed, he was only offering up the land *in case* the Vimy location didn't work out. The representative was fine with the original location, and always had been. Fletcher, furious, got in his van and left not long afterwards.

Two thousand eighteen turned to 2019 and somehow, we managed to win all four votes a second time—and yet it still wasn't over, because there was an appeal committee that met and discussed the project one last time on February 21, 2019.

The Friends of Sturgeon Creek, the organization that we'd already spoken with and assuaged that we wouldn't encroach on the creek, had actually hired a law firm to investigate the sale of the property. One of the things they claimed was that this was a backroom deal.

"*Back room?*" I said to Anne. "We went in through the front door and asked for help!"

We responded that the whole point of backroom deals was that someone came out of them making a bunch of money—and that obviously wasn't the case here. The only people who were going to profit from this centre were the people who would leave it with their lives back.

By that point we had so much momentum behind us, and I believe we'd successfully made the case that this was a legitimate and safe project. The appeal was voted unanimously against.

When the final vote went through, Anne and I were overjoyed. We'd now faced nine votes, and won them all.

The recovery centre had been a hotly contested issue, but now that it was done, we wanted to move on in a positive way. So, I wrote

a note to our supporters that was then posted to the Friends of Bruce Oake Facebook page.

"We cannot thank you enough for your unyielding support," the note read. "On our most discouraging days in this project it took one look at the 'Friends' page to know there was no turning back. Let's all try to remember one thing: while we celebrate today's vote we should not disparage those who opposed it. Hopefully, they will one day see the benefit of the Recovery Centre to society and their neighbourhood."

The idea was: it's time for us to all come together. We may not agree with the people who opposed the project, but we can at least respect their opinion.

That was the moment it all became real. We'd been mired in this bureaucratic process for nearly two years, and it was easy to sometimes lose focus on the point of it all: Bruce.

No matter what else was going on, in the end we were always a family who had lost a son to addiction. We never lost sight of that. The whole reason we were going to build this recovery centre was so that what happened to Bruce didn't have to happen to other people, and other people's children. It was going to be called the Bruce Oake Recovery Centre for a reason.

The Race to $15 Million

Winning that last vote was a beautiful moment, but it didn't last long. That evening, I lay in bed and a new worry jumped to the front of my mind: *how are we going to raise all of the money in time?*

When Anne and I first started talking to people about potential construction costs for the recovery centre, we anticipated it would cost around $7.5 million to build. By the time the plans came in for the actual design, however, we realized it would be double that amount—$15 million, give or take. The only way to raise that amount of cash was through a capital campaign.

Unofficially, our capital campaign had begun much earlier, since we'd already been raising money in various capacities. But we couldn't really announce it as such to the general public until we officially had the land, for obvious practical reasons.

There was also a perception issue to deal with. We were advised that, generally speaking, you want to have around 70 percent of your target amount already committed before you go public with your capital campaign. That way, people know that your goal is not just real, but already within reach. If you start at zero, people are less inclined to donate, because they won't believe you'll ever get there.

To help seed the ground, Marni had staged our first fundraising gala the previous August, right around the time of Bruce's birthday. As Marni often does, she turned the gala into a real hot ticket. It was called *Hockey Night in Canada—One Night Only*, and was hosted by Ron MacLean and Don Cherry. A number of the Winnipeg Jets players agreed to be there, and our guest of honour was Jonathan Toews, who on top of being a three-time Stanley Cup champion is also from Winnipeg. Darcy performed a compelling illusion for the crowd: a story with cards where the images on the cards added up to a picture of Bruce's face. The event sold out, and ended up raising more than $300,000 for us.

At that first gala, I was introduced to a guy named Ernie Waldner. He owned a number of companies, including a roofing and insulation business called Urecoat. I later met up with Ernie at the Manitoba Club, where he told me he wanted to donate the recovery centre's roof. I had no idea what something like that was worth, but it turned out to be around $500,000 in value. Ernie made this offer way in advance, when we were still a year and a half away from building the property—but when the time came, he stood by it.

When we had the land rezoned, Marni staged another gala on August 22, 2019—Bruce's birthday. It was another big night, emceed by Ron MacLean, Jann Arden, and Elliotte Friedman, with several NHL players and alumni in attendance. This gala raised another $350,000, and that doesn't count two unbelievable donations we received during the event.

One was when Bonnie and John Buhler went up to the microphone and announced to the room they were committing another $2 million on top of what they'd already donated. I couldn't believe my ears.

The second was when I was talking to a local businessman named Russ Edwards, whose son and daughter-in-law, Gary and Judy, I'd met a few weeks earlier. Gary and Judy were lovely people who had already donated $50,000 themselves, and they'd told us they were going to bring Russ with them to the gala. During dinner, after he'd learned about the project, Russ came over to me and said, "I'm going to give you a million bucks."

What do you say to something like that? My breath was taken away. I think I managed to get out, "Well, thank you very much!"

The next day was our sod-turning ceremony. Marni had a tent and two big signs set up out front of the site, and several of our major donors, including the Buhlers, were there in person. The funny part was that we couldn't turn any actual sod, because we hadn't gotten our demolition permit for the Vimy Arena yet. So we settled for sticking a few shovels into a big tub of dirt.

But it was a happy day nonetheless because we were finally able to announce our capital campaign to the media and the public. Thanks to the generosity of several major donors, we were already nearly 70 percent of the way to our goal. We had real momentum now, and we wanted to keep it going.

In Winnipeg, there are always three or four capital campaigns for big projects going on at any given time, and we were in competition with them. All of these other projects were worthwhile, of course, but there are only so many charitable dollars up for grabs, and we had to convince the public that our project was just as worthy of support as the others. We were incredibly fortunate to receive significant donations of both money and in-kind services, from vehicles to the food that would be served in the centre's cafeteria.

When we were first seriously starting to fundraise, in 2016, it had been difficult for us to land the really big-ticket donations—what are known in the fundraising world as "major gifts"—but Marni Larkin and Bob Kozminski, the chairman of our capital campaign, changed that for us through their vast connections. But it was also that now we had the land. Once we could point to an actual piece of property—one with big signs sticking out of the ground, announcing our intentions—it became much easier for people to buy into our vision. We weren't changing the pitch, but it was definitely being received more seriously now.

At first, I wasn't sure our campaign had a shot compared to the other ones that were going on at the time because in Winnipeg, it's the same people who get asked all the time for donations. The Buhlers, for instance, are first on everyone's list. But the craziest thing happened: Anne and I met with dozens of potential donors, and each time, they said yes. None of them—not one—ever said no to us. We always came away with something.

What worked in our favour, I think, was that most people we talked to recognized that addiction affects everyone, in one way or another—if not in their immediate household, then in their extended family or among their friends or coworkers. The other part is that people saw that Anne and I were a couple with no skin in the game, in terms of profit or self-interest. We were just trying to do the right thing.

The size of the amounts we were receiving could feel surreal at times, but it's funny how you become acclimatized to them, but Anne and I never lost our appreciation for donations of any amount. All along the way, we were still getting gifts of $50 and $100 at a time from individuals and families across Manitoba and beyond. At our first gala, in 2018, Anne read out loud the names of every family who'd sent in donations in the names of loved ones they'd lost to addiction. It was a long list—more than twenty names in all.

By December 2019, ten months after we'd won that last vote, our demolition permit came through, and the Vimy Arena was torn down. The following month, we started driving piles for the new recovery centre.

But long before construction began, we had to hire a builder. By this point, the Bruce Oake Recovery Centre was a high-profile project, so there was interest in it around the industry. Collectively, we came up with a shortlist of five companies, and for whatever reason, Bockstael Construction was not on it. I don't know why. Bockstael is a large, well-respected company that bills itself as Manitoba's builder, and it really is. They've built a lot of things around this province over the years.

One weekend I was in Vancouver to cover a game, and my phone rang as I was headed to my hotel. It was Darcy. He was hanging out

During demolition.

with his best friend, Anthony Militano, and it was obvious to me that they'd each had a beverage or two. Anthony's father, Carmine, was a senior executive at Bockstael, and Darcy and Anthony had decided that they had to be added to the shortlist. I heard them out and I had to admit they had a point.

When I got back into town, Anne, Darcy, and I had breakfast with Carmine and Anthony, and it was clear we'd overlooked them for no good reason. I asked Marni to add them to the list.

Later, when we went through all of the submitted proposals, it was obvious that Bockstael's was the best of the bunch. The thing that really jumped out at me about theirs was that they were going to pay for all of our preconstruction costs, which were significant. We already knew the company had a strong reputation and résumé. Plus, they really seemed to believe in the project. So we picked them for the job, and we never regretted it.

Meanwhile, we were also looking to hire our executive director. This was an incredibly important decision, as this person would be in charge of running the entire centre, both on a day-to-day basis and in terms of its long-term direction. Despite this, we didn't consult a headhunter. We didn't conduct an extensive international search, or even a national one. We just happened to have dinner with Greg Kyllo, who at the time was the Canadian Mental Health Association's national director of programs.

Marni had suggested to us to meet up with CMHA and seeing if there was some kind of partnership that could be forged between our two organizations. Despite working out of Toronto, Greg was originally from Manitoba and when he happened to be in town with his partner, Marion, we all met up.

At the same time, Bruce Holstead, from Fresh Start, was also in Winnipeg. We all met up as a group, and Bruce and Greg hit it off right away. Both are in long-term recovery themselves, and it just so happened that Greg had his thirteen-year sobriety medallion in his pocket, which Bruce countered with his own, this one for twenty years. There was an instant chemistry between them, as there often is for guys who are in long-term recovery, and we all had a great conversation. One thing that came up was Greg's interest in moving back to Winnipeg, should the right opportunity arise.

In November, just a month before the arena was demolished, Marni arranged a group dinner—she, Greg and Marion, and Anne and I—at Rae & Jerry's, a well-known local steakhouse. It's the kind of place where people go to see and be seen, and where a lot of business is conducted. We were probably there for two hours, most of which was spent listening to Greg telling us the story of his own recovery and how it had turned his life around. He told us he'd even played hockey at Vimy Arena as a kid—it was the site of his first-ever hockey fight.

Once the bill was paid, it was just Anne, Marni, and I sitting at our table. Marni asked us what we thought of Greg.

We said, "Let's hire him."

And that was it.

If you look at the situation in the abstract, this was no way to hire someone to run a company that would soon have thirty employees. But with Greg, we felt we'd hit the jackpot. Not only was he incredibly qualified, he was also a Winnipeg kid who knew exactly what long-term recovery meant. Greg really believed in our vision for the recovery centre, and the freedom he would have to help build a new model of treatment for Manitobans: providing a continuum of care, with no financial barriers.

Greg officially took over as our executive director in March 2020. That gave him enough time to wrap up his job with the CMHA, arrange to move across provinces, and also finish off his master's degree in social work while he was at it. For our part, we were just relieved to know that the job was filled. It would take time to start developing partnerships and drawing up our own version of the program—in fact, one of Greg's first tasks was flying to Calgary and shadowing the folks at Fresh Start for an entire week. He was employee number one at the Bruce Oake Recovery Centre, and from that point on would do all of the centre's future hiring himself.

If you ask Greg why he wanted the job so much, especially considering the prestigious gig at the CMHA he had to give up, his answer is always the same, without even thinking about it.

"I was willing to earn half as much to be twice as happy," he says.

Whenever people try to give Anne and me undue credit for our involvement in this whole project, I always say we were good at two things: having lunch and asking for money. The fact is that we were not called upon to do any of the heavy lifting, nor could we have done it *had* we been asked. I'm proud that we surrounded ourselves with a group of people who really knew what they were doing.

We had people like Marni, whose practical knowledge and experience changed everything for us. People like Bob Eastwood and Bob Kozminski, key members of our board. People like Leney Richardson, who runs all of the foundation's finances and helped get us set up with our bank. People like Ernie Waldner and the folks at Bockstael, who got the physical building built. And people like Greg, who used his expertise to make sure the recovery centre ran smoothly and effectively.

Once construction started, in January 2020, those people were all in place. So from that point onward, Anne and I weren't really faced with any big decisions. Instead, we could sit back and marvel as it all, finally, came together.

The only thing we didn't have, as the piles started going in, was all of the money committed. We were close, but not entirely there yet. Now, one school of thought will tell you that this was a terrible mistake. But Marni, Anne, and I all agreed we had to start right away. We were confident the rest of the money would come in time, so why wait? Plus, we were already getting calls, before there was even a hole in the ground, from people asking when we would be open, and how they could get on our waitlist. The need was just that high.

It was a leap of faith, no doubt. Some of our board members, I'm sure, probably would've preferred we waited until all of the money was actually in our bank account. But once again, it was Marni to the rescue. In the summer of 2020, with the COVID-19 pandemic in full swing, she helped us secure a grant from the provincial government for $3.5 million. That was what really brought the project home, and ensured that construction could continue uninterrupted. (Funnily enough, they paid us with an actual cheque, which I had to then bring to the bank. You ever try to deposit an amount that large? I can tell you the poor teller went a bit bug-eyed when he saw how many zeroes were on that thing.)

All told, construction on the recovery centre took about a year and a half. At the outset, we'd built four months' worth of delays into the timeline—and when COVID hit, we were extra grateful for the wiggle room. But when the folks at Bockstael handed us the keys, it was the end of April 2021—a full four months ahead of schedule. Despite all the logistical problems that came with operating during a pandemic, they'd been able to keep to the original schedule after all. This allowed Greg to start hiring staff, and Joe basically slept in the centre some nights, making sure that everything would be ready to go for our soft launch in May.

Anne and I were in and out of the site most days, giving tours to donors and politicians, but when we walked around the completed building for the first time, it was even more beautiful than we had imagined. The folks at Fresh Start had advised us to build a place where someone would want to live, and that's exactly what we'd ended up with. Our architects, MMP, nailed the design. The Bruce Oake Recovery Centre is a warm and inviting building, with tons of natural light spread across its fifty beds and 43,000 square feet. There are four classrooms for participants to work through the sixteen-week program—one of which has three of its four walls as floor-to-ceiling windows. The centre has an exercise room, several lounges and breakaway spaces, a full-sized gymnasium, and an industrial kitchen that serves up three healthy meals a day, free of charge, for participants and staff alike. On one side of the building, there is a beautiful view of Sturgeon Creek and the surrounding trail system. On the other, a friendly and well-kept neighbourhood. It really is serene—the kind of place Bruce would have loved.

During the design phase, Greg, Joe, and other members of the foundation worked hard on the interior of the building to make sure it followed modern best practices about helping folks in recovery. This included thinking about the building through the lens of trauma: using certain colours on the walls and organizing furniture in particular ways, in order to create an environment that feels healing and calm.

One of the most special areas is by the family room, where the Buhlers, in addition to their financial largesse to us, donated a series of prints of Sheila McGraw's illustrations from *Love You Forever*, Bruce's favourite book.

They also made sure the centre kept in mind the needs of the large Indigenous population in Manitoba. That's why, on the second floor on the centre, there is a special meditation and culture room, which includes a heavy-duty HVAC system that can accommodate the ceremonial burning of sacred medicine and plants. On the back patio, meanwhile, there is a sweat lodge and firepit for added cultural connection.

The most meaningful part of the building, however, is placed right at the entranceway. As soon as you enter the front doors, you are met by a wooden pillar with a glass case on top. This case features a photograph of Bruce, as well as the actual urn containing his remains.

I remember the day we took the urn out there. Anne, Darcy, and I brought it over with us from the gate-leg table in our family room, and we met up with Greg at the front entranceway of the centre. He asked everyone else to stay out of the room for a few minutes, and then we had a small dedication ceremony.

"God," I said out loud, "we commit Bruce to your eternal care and we pray you will help him guide this recovery centre to success."

The urn was placed there, in such a prominent position, as a reminder of both Bruce's story, and what's at stake for every participant who walks through our doors.

The Matriarch

Over the course of our marriage, Anne used to joke with me that she was fated not to make it past the age of sixty-five. It was a morbid joke, but not a totally unfounded one. Her mother died of a rare autoimmune disease called scleroderma, and her Aunt Joan died of ALS—another autoimmune disease—both at sixty-five years old. These were the two family members Anne was closest to in the world, and they both died from similar diseases at the exact same, relatively young age.

"It runs in the family!" she would tell me.

These were just passing comments, and I always dismissed them as such. "Come on, that's bullshit. You don't really believe it."

But in 2020, the year she turned sixty-four, Anne started getting sick. That fall she began losing weight and suddenly had very little appetite. It seemed like something wasn't right. I begged her, more than once, to go to the doctor and get herself checked out. But for months she resisted. "What are they going to tell me?" she'd always reply—which is probably the same thing I would've said, had our roles been reversed. She was as stubborn as I was.

This went on for a while, and in the new year, Anne's symptoms were still getting worse. But there was lots going on in our lives: the recovery centre was under construction, and we were busy thinking ahead to the opening. Finally, in February 2021, Anne felt so badly that she agreed to go to Emergency. It was a rare Saturday where I was actually at home, because we were in the middle of that compressed, COVID-related NHL season with the all-Canadian division. So I was there to drive her, and when she finally saw a doctor, it was thought to be a liver issue. From there, Anne was back and forth to her GP, who worked with Darcy's partner, Leslie, who is a doctor. After some time, she got an appointment with a specialist, who diagnosed her with primary biliary cholangitis, or PBC. This is a disease where the bile ducts in your liver are being slowly destroyed by your own immune system.

In short, another autoimmune disease.

This was a scary diagnosis on its own, especially because PBC has no known cure. But what made it worse for Anne was that it came during the pandemic. Her appointment with the liver specialist was in person at Health Sciences, but every other appointment she had with them was over the phone. Not even video. Just voices, talking about Anne's diagnosis and next steps without ever seeing one another in person.

At first, the doctor thought that with certain changes to her diet and lifestyle, Anne's liver might regenerate itself to some degree and she could continue living a good life that way. In that same time period she was admitted to hospital twice because her blocked liver ducts led to fluid pooling in her midsection, which she had to have tapped and drained. Each time litres of fluid would come out and she would immediately feel better. But even after making all of the doctor's suggested changes, she just kept getting weaker, and a transplant soon became the only viable option.

Her case was passed on to another specialist at Health Sciences, this time the doctor in charge of assessing people for liver transplants. The transplant surgeries were all done in Toronto, so our goal became to get Anne's name on the list and then keep it there. She went through a battery of tests to prove her need, and nobody who looked at the results ever disputed it.

Anne faced all of this with an admirable amount of optimism. She was up for the fight because she was determined to be part of the recovery centre, which was set to have its soft opening in May when the first clients would arrive. Anne's dream was to be at the centre every single day, working in the kitchen and generally being its matriarch. We were smart enough, as a couple, to know what we didn't know. Anne and I never got involved with decisions about programming or the like. But we probably called Greg on the phone three or four times per week, informally, just to hear about what was going on and ask what we could do to help. In the weeks before the opening, we conducted tours of the place with various politicians, government officials, and service groups—whoever wanted to come through, pretty much. Anne was able to drag herself to most of these tours, but she was increasingly fatigued.

In those final weeks of countdown, the recovery centre was a very busy place to be. Joe Leuzzi was running around at full speed, making sure everything was taken care of and that things were moving apace. Anne recruited her friends Kathy and Brenda to come and help her do laundry, putting sheets on the beds and getting fresh towels for the participants. But every once in a while, she had to go lie down on the nearest bed for fifteen or twenty minutes to get her energy back up.

On the day of the soft opening, Anne was determined to be there to meet the very first two guys who'd enrolled in the program. Their names were Shane and Rich, and they were both Manitobans dealing with opioids and meth. Both of them had also tried treatment in the past, but hadn't been successful. They were with us to try again. I remember, when we met them, they both expressed their gratefulness to Anne and me for getting the place built. For us, it was a big moment, because now it was real. The thing we'd been dreaming about was now happening. It's a bit of a cliché, but Anne and I really believed it: if we could save even one person's life, it would all be worth it.

In the coming days more and more guys would show up, and we got to meet all of them, too.

It was important for Anne to be around as much as she could in those early days, and the only limiting factor was her health. One day we were walking past the gymnasium, where our trainer Derek was putting a half-dozen guys through a pretty intense workout. As soon as he saw us, Derek got the guys to stop exercising and applaud us. It was one of many meaningful moments, and I was so glad that Anne could be there to experience them.

Meanwhile, we were trying to keep some semblance of a normal life going. The cottage in the Whiteshell was Anne's favourite place on earth, so when the weather got warmer we tried to spend as much time there as we could. We'd had it remodelled a few years earlier, and it was always a great place to relax and spend time together. But this year Anne was having trouble enjoying herself.

One day in July, she started having piercing abdominal pain and collapsed onto the floor. I was outside, and couldn't hear her because she'd become so weak she couldn't physically yell anymore—she'd lost probably thirty pounds by this point. I helped her up onto the bed and tried to get her comfortable, but the pain wouldn't go away. Anne was a pretty tough lady, so I knew whatever was stopping her in her tracks must be serious.

I got her into the car and we drove straight back to Winnipeg. I was scared, but did my best to keep things together and deal with this latest problem head-on, just like we always had. On the way I called her GP, who told me we needed an ambulance. At this point we'd already made it back to our house, so I went inside and called 911. The operator asked me what the emergency was. I said my wife was really sick and needed an ambulance. They asked if she was conscious, and I said yes, but just barely. Then she said someone would call us back shortly.

"What do you mean *shortly?*" I asked.

"Within the next forty-five minutes," the operator said.

Anne was still in excruciating pain, and, finally, a paramedic called back about twenty minutes later. I quickly realized he had a very specific job: to try to talk us *out* of needing an ambulance. Now, that wasn't his fault. As is the case in a lot of Canadian cities these days, there was a queue of people who needed help, and not enough ambulances to go around. But it was still an incredibly frustrating circumstance to suddenly find ourselves in.

"Look," the guy said, "is there any way we can resolve this without an ambulance?"

I said, "I know what you're really asking: *can't I just send her in a cab, or take her in myself?*"

I wasn't losing it, but it was a circular conversation with no end in sight. And the truth was, I didn't feel comfortable putting Anne back in our car. She was in that much pain. I wanted an ambulance to keep her safe and comfortable, and to bring her right up to the doors of the hospital so that everyone would know she needed help, fast.

Fortunately, at that moment Leslie came into the house. I gave the phone to her, and she used her medical expertise to more accurately describe Anne's condition, and thereby talk the operator into keeping her in the queue. Thank God, the ambulance showed up sooner rather than later.

Anne was admitted to hospital, and once again they took three or four litres of fluid out of her midsection before discharging her a few days later. But she was still weak. From there we transitioned into several more phone calls with the liver specialist, always with the goal of keeping her as high on the transplant list as possible. In the meantime, there were always new tests to take and forms to fill out.

Back at the recovery centre, Marni had scheduled the formal opening for Bruce's birthday, on August 22, 2021. But Anne just kept getting sicker.

It was getting so bad now that I managed to get us another phone appointment with the transplant specialist at Health Sciences. Anne and I were sitting at our kitchen table, and we had him on speakerphone. I basically begged him, "Can you please see her in person? I think if you saw her, you'd realize that something needs to be done right now." But COVID protocols were still in effect, and it was seen as too risky for everyone involved.

A few days later, on August 20, she was looking even worse. Anne was still trying to downplay her symptoms, but again I couldn't stay silent. We agreed she couldn't come to the formal opening looking and feeling the way she did. She could barely walk and was having trouble staying awake. I called an ambulance again—but this time I knew how the game was played. When they asked me if she was conscious, I said no. This wasn't technically true, but it wasn't far off, either. Sure enough, this time the ambulance came right away.

Even when she was first admitted, we were hopeful that it was simply a matter of draining more fluid, and that maybe she'd be released in time to attend the opening. But that was probably always unrealistic. In the end, she watched the opening of the Bruce Oake Recovery Centre from her hospital bed, on Facebook Live, with Debbie at her side.

The next day, August 23, the doctors drained more fluid from Anne—but this time they took so much that there was what's called a fluid shift, and her blood pressure cratered. The following morning, Anne went to stand up and collapsed. I got a call from the hospital, telling me what had happened and letting me know she was being moved to the ICU. I rushed over right away to see her. Anne was awake and alert, but she was extremely weak. The first thing the doctors did was pump her full of fluids again. I stayed with her for the rest of the day.

The day after that, we had an interview with the liver specialist in Toronto who was in charge of admissions. Anne was lucid and presented well, and the doctor told us that she was a prime candidate for a transplant. The plan was to get her to Toronto as soon as her blood pressure went back to normal.

We'd already begun the process of finding a donor, and Darcy was even a potential option, because his O negative blood is compatible with all other blood types. But we were learning that Anne's case was progressing so quickly that there likely wouldn't be time to find a living donor. Instead, her only option was a deceased liver—in other words, if someone were to die as the result of a car crash or other kind of accident, and they were an organ donor with the right blood type, that's the liver Anne would get.

Despite the setbacks, we both left that conversation feeling hopeful. Compared to her other issues, blood pressure seemed like a relatively simple one to fix.

Unfortunately, in trying to restore Anne's lost fluids, the doctors ended up giving her so much that it spilled over into her lungs. I'd barely made it home that night from our interview with the liver specialist when the hospital called to say that Anne was now having trouble breathing, and so was being put on bilevel positive airway pressure (also called BiPap). This involves breathing through a giant oxygen mask and is basically a less invasive type of ventilator. But then when that didn't work, they had to fully intubate her.

When I got back to the hospital, the nurse who was on shift warned me to get ready, that I might not like what I see. Sure enough,

I started crying as soon as I saw Anne with those tubes down her throat. We were told the intubation was a temporary fix, just for a couple of days, until her lungs started to dry out. But the tubes were still in when Anne woke up, four days later. The tube in her throat meant she couldn't talk, but she had a notepad and pen next to her bed, and the first thing she wrote was, "Let me go." It was almost too much to bear.

COVID restrictions were still in place, so Anne could only have one visitor at a time. Darcy, Debbie, and I would take turns being with her, and it was hard for all of us. Darcy in particular struggled with seeing his mother in such a vulnerable state, to the point where he found it difficult to be in the same room with her. The other factor was that his wife, Leslie, was three months pregnant at the time. Darcy told Anne she had to keep fighting because she was going to be a grandmother. In all, the tube stayed in for about a week.

Finally, Anne recovered enough that one of the doctors did a few tests to make sure she could breathe on her own. Then, finally, they took the tube out. Her throat was so sore that she could barely speak. The first thing she did was turn to Darcy, who had been scared to be near her when she was intubated, and, smiling, whispered, "Chickenshit."

The day they took that tube out was one of the happiest days of my life. I thought we were home free. I really did. When I went back to the hospital parkade to get my car that afternoon, I saw it had been broken into. The driver-side door and window were all beat up. I couldn't have cared less. That tube coming out was the only thing that mattered.

But that night the doctors called again, and said Anne was having more trouble breathing on her own than they expected. They put her back on BiPap, and the next morning they had to reintubate her. As part of that process they knocked her out.

It was another punch to the gut. I managed to get through that weekend in part by leaning on my brother Stuart, who is a longtime urologist in Ottawa. He was the one who first said to me, gently, that I might need to think about making a hard decision here, in case Anne didn't recover.

The next day—Monday, September 6—I went up to the hospital and asked the doctor, "Is there any hope here?" He told me he had to be honest: Anne's organs were already showing signs of failure. That was all I needed to hear. I knew Anne didn't want to be kept in that state, and she would've wanted all of the medical resources expended on her be used on someone else instead.

I went home and gathered up Darcy, Leslie, Debbie, and Stuart (who'd flown in to be with us).

"It's over," I said to them.

Darcy was distraught, understandably, and Debbie and Stuart did their best to console him.

"She's not there anymore," Debbie told him. "She's already gone."

The doctors had told me, before I left, how the procedure would work. They assured me that Anne would pass away quickly and peacefully. There wouldn't be any pain. It was tough, but eventually Darcy agreed. We all knew what we had to do. I called the hospital and said we were coming.

Before we pulled the plug, Darcy asked me to leave the room. He then took his mother's hand and put it on Leslie's stomach one last time.

After it was done, I sat with Anne at her bedside until it was over. In our final moments together I just tried to comfort her, and whispered to her that it was okay to go. Anne was a woman of very strong faith, and she'd always said that death didn't scare her, because it meant she would finally see Bruce again. I reminded her of that, too. She truly believed that Bruce was waiting for her in the afterlife, and if that helped her in those final days, then God bless her.

By midafternoon she was gone. She died at age sixty-five, essentially, from drowning. Her lungs never got dry.

Thirteen

Guiding Light

After Anne passed, I called Marni—as I always did in difficult situations—and told her I wanted to have a celebration of life for Anne. And I wanted it held at the recovery centre.

I also asked her, in between my blubbering, to send out a press release, in which Anne was referred to specifically as the matriarch of the Bruce Oake Recovery Centre. It became a real news story. Her death was reported in local newspapers, and the mayor and premier both issued statements of condolence. Everyone knew Anne was a driving force behind the recovery centre, and it was her persistence that led, in no small way, to getting it built.

Marni suggested Ron MacLean as a possible emcee for the ceremony, and I agreed immediately. It had to be him. In addition to being a valued colleague at *Hockey Night in Canada*, Ron is a truly wonderful man who's always been in Anne's and my corner. We called him with barely three days' notice, and he was there with no hesitation. A bunch of my other colleagues came, too: Elliotte Friedman, Kelly Hrudey, Chris Cuthbert, Kerrin Lee-Gartner, and several producers I'd worked with over the years. It was really touching to see all of those familiar faces in the crowd.

We intentionally called it a celebration of life, not a funeral, so there were a lot of happy memories and stories shared that day. Darcy spoke, as did Anne's friends Debbie, Brenda, and Kathy, as well as two people whose lives Anne had basically saved by helping them when they were at their lowest ebbs. The whole event was about an hour long—and this, too, was a nod to Anne. We'd always joked with one another about how much we hated events where the speeches droned on for hours and hours. So I made sure this one was in accordance with both of our limited attention spans.

In my public speaking over the years, I've always said, "God acted kindly when He brought Anne and me together." She was such a special person, and the sad fact was that we all lost a caring and compassionate soul that day. Anne and I used to talk all the time about how the point of life was to use our time on this earth to make a difference. This whole ceremony underlined that Anne had succeeded in that mission.

It was a beautiful event, and it was incredibly meaningful to be able to host it in the building that Anne and I had spent so many years dreaming of. Darcy, Marni, and Greg all agreed that it had to be held at the recovery centre.

On top of overseeing the plan for the centre for so many years, Marni helped bury Anne. I don't know how many funerals she's had to organize in her career, but she organized this one to a tee. I could never pay her back for that—or for everything else she's done for me over the years.

The celebration of life took place on Saturday, September 11. The first group of participants from the recovery centre was set to graduate the following week.

The Bruce Oake Recovery Centre had its grand opening on August 22, 2021—the date that should have been Bruce's thirty-sixth birthday.

"We're happy today that Bruce's spirit is alive and well in this beautiful place of healing," I told the media who came to cover the event. "Bruce, you are our guiding light in this beautiful project. You got us this far, and I know you're going to take us the rest of the way."

I was there with Darcy, and we were both emotional wrecks, in part because Anne wasn't able to be there with us. But amidst our personal grief, it was hard not to be inspired by all of the work happening around us.

A few weeks later, the centre celebrated its first graduating class. In those first days after Anne's death, Darcy, Leslie, and I all hunkered down at home together. They actually stayed in the house for a few extra weeks, just to make sure I was okay. I was, but I liked having them around, so I didn't move to kick them out too quickly.

Greg asked if I would come speak at the graduation ceremony, and at first I demurred. I didn't want to become the centre of attention, and I didn't want people to feel sorry for me. But he insisted it was what everyone wanted, so eventually I agreed.

Like the celebration of life, we held the graduation in the gymnasium of the recovery centre. It's full of natural light, with a huge window overlooking the stage, on which we'd set up a lectern and a microphone. On the gym floor were rows of folding chairs set up for the graduates, their families, and their friends.

I made my way up to the stage for the second time that week, and looked out at the joyful faces in the crowd, all of whom felt hopeful for the future in a way they hadn't in a very long time. These guys were excited to get back into the world, and, through my grief, I wanted nothing more than for all of them to succeed at doing just that.

"We said goodbye to my wife, the matriarch of this place, a few days ago," I said into the microphone. "It was her dream to see people succeed in their sobriety. We know it's a lot of work, but I ask you today to honour her memory—and Bruce's memory—by doing that work. Thank you."

It must have been one of the shortest speeches I've ever given in my life. But I heard applause ringing in my ears as I went back to my seat and sat down. Had she been there to see it, I know Anne would've been just as proud of those guys as I was.

Greg had ramped up admissions to get Bruce Oake to capacity as quickly as possible. The centre has fifty beds, but it wasn't as simple as letting in the first fifty guys on the waitlist. In order to make sure there's no bottleneck—both in terms of admissions and graduations—you have to space them out over the sixteen-week process.

The first two guys came in on May 25, and by the end of July, every bed was full. This was faster than even Greg had thought possible—he was expecting the process to last well into the fall. It may have felt a bit rushed in those early months, but there was so much need in the community that every bed was snapped up as soon as it became available.

There was urgency when the project began, and much more urgency by the time it opened, thanks to the pandemic. COVID-19 really exacerbated the crisis the centre was trying to respond to. Many other services around the province were shutting down, so the resources people were accessing normally suddenly weren't available anymore. Most of the usual twelve-step meetings were closed. Then you add to that the fact that people were living in isolation, unable to go outside and do the things they normally did. You couldn't even leave your house at some points. That's an invitation for bad habits to creep back in, because isolation is one of the things that kills people in recovery. Those are the times where people struggle the most.

Really, the opioid crisis had become its own pandemic, when you consider the number of overdose deaths per year in Canada—more than 7,000 in 2022 alone, according to the federal government. In most provinces, overdose is a leading cause of premature death, or death under the age of fifty. That is staggering.

None of us were naïve enough to think that this one recovery centre was going to fix the problem. But we knew it would help, and it has.

Plenty of people have told me since the opening that Bruce Oake has changed the landscape of recovery in Manitoba. Before 2021, if people in the province wanted a treatment program with this level of

detail and care, they'd have to look elsewhere and then figure out a way to get there. Now, they just have to get here. Word gets around quickly when you have a reputation as sterling as Bruce Oake's already has, and Greg tells me that he routinely hears from people across the country, from B.C. to the Maritimes.

There's a stat out there that if you take a high-flying addict off the streets and keep them sober for a year, it can save taxpayers as much as $100,000. That might sound like a lot, but it really isn't hard to reconcile when you consider the decreased demand on police, the courts, social services, and the health-care system. Hell, one critical visit to the hospital can end up costing the system upwards of $25,000.

In its first full year of operation, the Bruce Oake Recovery Centre worked with approximately 200 men. Of those, 152 made it through the waiting period and were admitted to treatment, and 100 were able to complete the full, sixteen-week program. You hear a lot in recovery about a given centre's "success rate." For Bruce Oake, that means the percentage of graduates who go on to achieve at least one year of sobriety, and in that first year it was 57 percent—among the highest success rates anywhere in Canada.

So let's do the math. Fifty-seven men at $100,000 a pop is $5.7 million. That's how much money this centre potentially put back into the pockets of taxpayers in its first year alone.

Also, that number doesn't include other economic benefits, like the fact that people who graduate then return to being working, contributing members of society. There are other statistics out there that say for every dollar you invest in addiction treatment and recovery, society gets back as much as $15 in return. So even if you only look at the centre in purely economic terms, it provides a fantastic return on its investment.

And that's *also* not counting all of the intangible things that the participants themselves receive on the other side of sobriety. This is sometimes called the social return on investment, and its effect is just as real. At our graduation ceremonies, the majority of the guys up on that stage will specifically talk about how sobriety has made them better fathers, better spouses, and better children to their own parents. Their quality of life improves immeasurably in recovery, and the connections that are restored between them and their family, friends, and overall community are quite literally priceless.

There are plenty of other stats I could show you to quantify the good work being done at Bruce Oake every day. In that first year, for instance, 13 percent of participants had jobs at the time they were admitted, and just 27 percent of them had stable housing. One year after graduating from treatment, those numbers jumped to 83 percent and 97 percent, respectively. It's an incredible change—and these are sustained, long-term impacts. The program at Bruce Oake isn't just about getting sober but also about all of the things that being sober gives you: a place to live, a place to work, and being around the people you love. Those are the reasons people get sober in the first place. That's how you live a full, productive life.

There's a lot of talk across Canada these days about reconciliation with Indigenous peoples, but it's more than talk at Bruce Oake. It informs everything they do, and has since day one. Forty percent of the participants at Bruce Oake are Indigenous, and everyone has the opportunity to engage in their cultural practices—whether that's smudging, or sweat lodges, or any others. Those benefits extend to

non-Indigenous participants, too, because they have the chance to live alongside Indigenous and learn about the harms that were done to their ancestors, which still have an impact in the present day. Greg always says that one of the benefits of recovery is that it doesn't discriminate: despite their differences, everyone who comes in the centre's doors is dealing with a common problem and pushing towards a common solution. There's a real bond between participants that lasts long after they graduate.

Greg and his staff have given tours of the facility to a lot of people, including some well-known politicians and public figures. The number-one thing they hear is: "I didn't know what to expect, but I wasn't expecting *this*." Visitors are consistently blown away by how beautiful the building is, but also how clean and tidy everything is. And do you want to know the secret? They don't have any cleaners. A big part of recovery is learning everyday skills and taking responsibility for your own life, so every day the participants are given different chores to do, from cleaning bathrooms to helping in the kitchen. The guys take real pride in their work, because this is their home, and it shows. In fact, the one day Greg did hire professional cleaners was for the grand opening—and it was a waste of money! Because the building didn't look any cleaner than it does on any other day of the week.

The Bruce Oake Recovery Centre does incredible work, and in the process, it's won over many of the more hesitant residents in the neighbourhood. Through a variety of outreach programs, they've seen that not only is there nothing to fear from the centre, but also that it's doing a tremendous amount of good. (The centre has also won over multiple insurance companies, who now cover the entire sixteen-week program for people on disability. That speaks volumes to the faith that other organizations have in the program—because insurance companies don't give money away, I can assure you.) I'm confident that anyone who takes the time to really learn about addiction and recovery would feel the same way.

At the same time, everyone at Bruce Oake, from the staff to the participants, knows that this centre is only the first step in a very long battle against a very difficult disease. We don't need one Bruce Oake Recovery Centre—we need nine or ten, and that's just in Manitoba. Obviously, not everyone who loses someone to addiction is going to go out and raise $15 million to build a centre themselves, the way that Anne and I were lucky enough to. But if, having finished reading this book, you care about this issue and want to do something about it, there are several things you can do.

First of all, you can help us change people's mindsets about addiction in general. We want the public to recognize that addiction is a medical condition. More specifically, addiction is a chronic brain disorder—and a fucking awful one at that. It's got to be one of the only diseases that tells you you don't have a disease. I once overheard Greg talking with someone who was adamant that addiction was a choice, and he asked her, "Well, what would make someone choose vodka over their kids?" I mean, just think about that for a second. Anyone who chooses alcohol over their family obviously has a brain that's not wired properly. That isn't a rational decision. Which means that addiction isn't a moral failure: it's a health issue.

As a society, we need to greet people who are struggling with addiction—whether they're secretly drinking on the job, or passed out in front of the local Safeway—with compassion. Nobody wants to be in those situations, least of all them. Who would actively choose that kind of life? Everyone who's been through Bruce Oake can answer that question: nobody.

Another thing you can do is lobby all levels of government—local, provincial, and federal—to invest more into treatment. I've been very disappointed in the last few federal elections that addiction recovery and treatment was not part of any party's major platform. If you look at the statistics, you cannot tell me that this shouldn't be a national priority. Addiction and overdose is an issue that needs leadership from the highest levels in this country. When I see that kind of indifference across the board, I despair.

I've said it before, and I'll keep saying it: we are currently leaving a generation of addicts out there to die. But it doesn't need to be that way.

Also, if you've read this book and believe in its message, you can help spread the word about what may be the single most important piece of information for people to hear: *treatment for addiction exists.* A lot of people simply don't know that there's a solution out there, but high-quality, evidence-based treatment is real, and it's available. Without that knowledge, a lot of people who are struggling lose hope, and they don't take action as a result.

To be honest, Greg and the staff at Bruce Oake deal with this scepticism even among some of the guys who show up at the building. And I get it: these are guys who've been through so many challenges, hurdles, and bureaucratic problems in their lives, just to try to seek treatment and turn their lives around. So when they see this beautiful facility, with expert staff, natural light, comfortable beds, cultural amenities, and three square meals each day—and they hear that the treatment works—*and* that it's all free—some of them simply don't believe it. They assume there has to be a catch somewhere. But there isn't.

The model is real, it works, and it can work in your city, too, if you want it to.

In reading this book, I hope it's clear that Bruce, for all of his troubles, wasn't a monster. He had a disease, and it ultimately claimed his life. But addiction is not a moral failing. It also doesn't play favourites. I mentioned earlier that the Bruce Oake Recovery Centre has a series of Sheila McGraw's prints from Robert Munsch's *Love You Forever* on its walls, and you wouldn't believe the number of guys who look at those illustrations and say, "My mother used to read me that book all the time."

Which is a reminder that all people—including addicts—are somebody's child.

Anne and I have always said that we would give everything we have for one more day with Bruce. We'll never have that, so instead the recovery centre is where his legacy will carry on. I'm so proud to know that it's already saving lives, and changing the face of recovery in Manitoba in the process. I can't think of a better place to bear his name.

When the Bruce Oake Recovery Centre first opened, there was one minor but recurring criticism: why was it only for men? Well, the short answer is because it's not a good idea to mix men and women together

when they're at their most vulnerable. You can take every precaution, from barbed wire to tasers, and they'll still find each other. At which point the conversation becomes, "We don't need this place. We have each other." Unfortunately, recovery doesn't work that way.

But the criticism had a point. We always agreed that women suffer from addiction just as strongly as men do, and are just as deserving of the same barrier-free access to treatment. That's why I'm proud to say that plans are already underway for our second treatment facility in Winnipeg: the Anne Oake Family Recovery Centre.

The goal with Anne Oake is to provide a treatment experience that's just as high-quality as the one offered at Bruce Oake, but tailored for women's specific needs. Most importantly, it has "family" in the title because a lot of women are afraid that if they go into recovery, they're going to lose their kids to government care. Here, we will do everything we can so that women will be able to have their kids with them. If all goes to plan, the new centre will include a full day care, plus specialized counselling services and larger bedrooms with enough space for moms and their young children.

Because of those factors, the new centre is going to cost a lot more to build than Bruce Oake did. But we're up for the fight. In fact, we've already secured several million dollars in new donations, and all of the major donors we've spoken with are behind us. With the support of Premier Wab Kinew and the Manitoba government, we've also acquired a choice piece of property in the South End of Winnipeg. In September 2024, we officially announced our new capital campaign and held a groundbreaking ceremony on the site of the new centre. Bruce Oake runs mortgage-free because we were able to raise all of our funds ahead of time. We'd love to do the same with Anne Oake.

Groundbreaking day for the Anne Oake Family Recovery Centre (from left to right): Ron MacLean, Premier Wab Kinew, Josh Morrissey, Scott Oake, Darcy Oake and daughter August, Gary Doer, and Elders Jim Bear and Alix Roussin.

Ultimately, the Anne Oake Family Recovery Centre, like Bruce Oake before it, will get built because it has to. The demand for recovery is only growing, and women deserve the same opportunities that men have. It just makes sense.

And it's even more fitting that the new centre will be built in memory of Anne, who was the matriarch not just of our family but also the Bruce Oake Centre as a whole. Once it's complete, her legacy will live on forever—right alongside Bruce's.

Epilogue

The Story of Terrence

The guys who walk through the doors of the Bruce Oake Recovery Centre come from all backgrounds and all walks of life. So I wanted to end this book with the story of one of the centre's most exceptional graduates: Terrence Morin, who left behind a life of violent crime and gang activity for a life of sobriety—and, more recently, a job at Bruce Oake as a resident support worker. (You may also remember him from the prologue of this book, where he told the new graduates, "Recovery is real. Brotherhood is real.")

When we first met, in 2021, I asked Terrence where he'd come in from, and he said the provincial jail. I asked what he'd been in for, and he started listing all of these things he'd done. It was a long list—he probably got halfway through before I had to say, "Okay, Okay, that's enough!"

At first, Terrence presented to me like someone who wasn't quite sure he wanted to be here. Again, I'm no expert in recovery, but my feeling about him was that he might be 50-50. But he quickly took to the place, and before long became a Senior Peer here, helping the next generation of guys embrace sobriety the way he has. Now he has a full-time job. There's not much any participant can say to Terrence that he hasn't gone through himself. And if a guy with his background can accomplish what he's accomplished, then anybody can. That's what he represents. He's a valuable, valuable resource for Bruce Oake.

Take it away, Terrence.

My institutional record is violent. Even though my whole time in jail, I was good. I didn't get into no fights. I worked as a barber, so they trusted me with scissors. But I had a step-one problem. One of my baby mamas told me I needed help. She was familiar with the twelve steps, and she told me I had a problem admitting I had a problem. She told me, "You've never admitted anything. You're always in denial."

There were two months left in my time in jail, and I wasn't sure what I should do. One night we were watching the 10 o'clock news, and there was a story about Bruce Oake. I was like, "What is this place?" I knew exactly where it was. I grew up in this neighbourhood: my mom lived in this neighbourhood, my sister lived in this neighbourhood. It was like something was telling me: *you need help, dog.* I was so eager to wake up the next morning and call.

I met Scott on my first day here. I was coming from jail, and I seen the gym. I had a routine to work out every day, but I hadn't worked out that day yet, because I was up early getting released. They gave me a tour, and when I saw the gym, I thought, *This is going to be one of my favourite rooms here.* So I was working out, and I saw Scott. I didn't know who he was. I thought he was one of the participants.

Coming from that jail mentality, where you don't really make eye contact, I saw him and thought, *Okay, this guy is pumping some weights here.* But I didn't say anything. I just minded my own business. Obviously I was nervous, too. It was a new environment.

Later, I asked some people, "Yo, who is that guy?"

They were like, "That's Scott Oake!"

I'm like, "Oh, shoot."

The next day I introduced myself. I said to him, "You're the guy who made this all happen?" He said yeah, but then he told me about Bruce, and how when guys come in, they walk past Bruce's urn. I was addicted to the same thing Bruce was addicted to. It's a powerful drug, a powerful addiction. So now every time I walk by his urn, I say, "What's up, homie?" Like he's right there. I heard he was a rapper, so I know he had some powerful words. He probably had that swag, too.

When I first got here, I was close-minded. I would go to the gym, then back to my room. I would eat, then go back to my room. I was used to that confinement. I didn't really talk to anyone in my first month and a half. I had to restart the program, too, because I wasn't doing what I was supposed to be doing. I was hiding out. I wasn't engaging in the activities. When it was my turn to speak, I would pass.

It was weird, because everyone was shaking my hand. A couple guys tried to hug me. I was like, "Whoa, what the heck?" I wasn't used to that yet. I thought these guys were fake, and I've seen a lot of fakeness in my life. These alumni kept messaging me—"How are you doing?"—and it was weird to get all these messages from guys I didn't know.

What clicked for me was when I changed counsellors, and met Eddie—me and him have the exact same birthday, on the exact same year. I don't know about the time. So when he was getting born in Grace Hospital, I was getting born in Thompson, Manitoba. There was that connection between us. I needed a guy to call me on my shit. "Did you do your steps? Did you do your work? Did you go to your meetings?" I did all that, and I became a Senior Peer here.

I was surprised when they hired me, too. I don't know how to explain it. I wanted to cry, but I didn't want to cry.

I was like, "Are you sure? I got no education. I got nothing."

They said, "You have life experience."

I was like, "Yo, I'm down. This place saved my life. I'll be a foot soldier for this place forever."

I'm a residence support worker, so that means I do room checks. I'm almost like a CO [corrections officer]. I'll look in every room, and I talk to everyone. "How are you doing, bro? You doing good? You going to your meetings?" I'll tell them if we have sweat lodges coming up, ask if they have a sponsor, stuff like that.

I want to be a positive leader. I'm a member of the Pukatawagan First Nation. It's a fly-in reserve between Flin Flon and Le Pas, right on the border of Saskatchewan. When I was here, I got my spirit name, and I got in tune with my culture. The knowledge keeper here gave me my spirit name: Nagani maiingan, which means *leading wolf*.

They said I have signs of being a leader, and that if I do the right thing, people will follow me. That helps me as much as it helps them.

I know that out of thirty guys, five of them are listening to me. Maybe the rest aren't there yet, but I'll be there when they get there. I'm not forcing anyone to follow me. But whatever's been shown to me, I'll throw it their way. Because I was like that when I was a new guy.

I tell the guys, "Recovery is real." That's my slogan. The twelve steps in this place connected with me, and they helped me connect to my higher power. So that's what I say now: we're spiritual gangsters. It depends how you define *gangster*, but for me, the most gangster shit I ever did in my whole life was turn my life around. I got educated—I just got my GED. Now I'm going to college in the fall to become an addictions counsellor. This place, and the supports and the culture they have here, made me who I am today.

There's some stuff I regret in my past. But I don't regret all of it, because I'm a survivor—of addiction, of gang life, of the street life. Now I can use that to be the example. It doesn't matter what colour or background you are. Recovery is real. If you want it, you can get it. But you can't just pray. You have to work for it. In a gang, you have a code of conduct. There are rules. So I use that for the twelve steps here—those are my new code of conduct. That's what's going to keep me sober today, and keep me sober tomorrow. This is my lifestyle now.

I did the program, so I can say to guys, "I've been exactly where you are. I was shy, I was nervous. Just keep an open mind to this place." That camaraderie that we speak about, it's real. Now, I hug and shit. It's a safe spot. Like, "I care about you, bro. You don't know me yet, but by the end of this program, I'm going to be your brother.

If someone's messing around with you, or you're having a hard time, message me." We've all got something in common.

For a long time in my life, all I had to talk about was being in jail, stuff I'd done, this and that. I didn't try to glorify it, but it's all I had. Now I've flipped that negativity into a positive. It got me where I am today, and gave me more motivation and determination to not ever go back to that lifestyle. It used to be, "Let's go steal this fucking car!" Now it's, "Let's go to this meeting, bro!" Let's go play baseball, or basketball. Let's go work out.

I've been to a few other treatment centres, but there's nothing like this place. I like that it's an all-male facility. At other treatment centres there were females there, too, and it was a distraction. I couldn't be me, because I was always trying to be what a girl wants me to be. No disrespect to co-ed treatment centres, but at those places I left with a girl, and now I have a kid with her. Here, it's that brotherhood, that camaraderie. I tell these guys, "We're like a gang, but we all want the same thing."

When I went back to school, I got a conscientious award—I don't even know what that means. My mom passed away from an OD, too. I remember her telling me, "If you come home one day and give me that diploma, I'll be so proud of you." I wasn't the best son. But I'm trying to honour a lot of people who fell in that addiction life—Bruce, a couple of guys here, my mom, everybody that's on the street. That could've been me. That *was* me. I overdosed a few times, but I got brought back.

When I OD'd, I woke up and was like, "What happened?"

They said, "You just died, bro."

It felt like nothing. I didn't want to be that nothing—that statistic.

I'm going to Yellowquill College, which is close by, to be an addictions counsellor and mental health worker. It's a two-year program, but what's two years, man? I'm thirty-six years old, and I've spent the majority of my life in and out of jail. I'm down. And I just live a couple streets over from Bruce Oake—it's 587 steps away. I counted. So there's no need for me to be late for work.

Our knowledge keeper here is Ojibwe, so I've been following the Ojibwe teachings. It's the same thing, right? I'm down to learn anything about my culture, anything that's spiritual. I'm like a sponge. I used to be a grass dancer when I was younger, but I lost my way. So I just got my new grass-dancing outfit made, and I'm starting to dance again. I'm a sundancer, and an ogichidaa dancer. That means *warrior.* My whole life, I thought a warrior had to be violent. But a warrior just means a man with a big heart. Someone who's ready to protect their people. That's why I got this tattoo on my face. It's my war paint. I go to war every day—with myself, some days. I'm going to fight for my recovery, you know what I mean?

They say to make amends to your family for what you did wrong. But my counsellor told me to first wait a year from graduation, *then* go to your people and tell them you changed your life. Don't do it right away, because they aren't going to believe you. Show them through action. So I went back to school, and I wrapped my diploma around the box with my mom's ashes in it. It was like it was hugging her. That's what she wanted.

I'm going to honour my mom, I'm going to honour all of the people who've fallen to addiction, and I'm going to use my story to help these people and help myself. I don't ever want to go back to that fucking life. Because I remember all of those dark, lonely times when I

was by myself, and I'd try to go and ask for help, and nobody believed me. I'd go to treatment, and then I'd take off.

This place showed me that I can die tomorrow if I make the wrong decision. The stuff I was addicted to can kill me. It killed Bruce. It's no joke—and there I was, joking around for most of my life. I don't want to do that no more.

When new guys come in, I tell them, "This is Bruce's house. He's here with us. Don't disrespect it."

I got one of those jerseys hanging from the rafters of the gym with my name on it. That's a trip, too. In five years I'm going to come back and get it.

Acknowledgements

Any parent will understand the significant challenge in writing this book. Reliving some of Bruce's behaviour was extraordinarily difficult, especially his struggle with addiction. I've often thought if only I knew then what I know now about addiction or substance abuse, would it have made a difference in his journey? Perhaps not, but it would have made me more compassionate and understanding.

Technically I wrote this book. Practically speaking I spoke gibberish to Michael Hingston for hours on end. Michael took my streams of consciousness and turned them into English. I am indebted to him and to my editors Sarah St. Pierre, Grace O'Connell, and Jim Gifford for the care they applied to what they consistently called "this important book."

There would be no Bruce Oake Recovery Centre and there will be no Anne Oake Family Recovery Centre without community. Anne, Darcy, and I saw every dollar donated as a vote in favour of treatment and recovery, from twenty dollars on up to gifts in the millions. It wasn't a hard sell largely because of the devastating reach of addiction. It may not be in your home. It could be somewhere in your family tree, and it is definitely in your wallet.

I shall be eternally grateful to Bonnie and John Buhler for giving the project life. It is a long list of benevolent and compassionate citizens and organizations who gave and continue to give from the heart—too long to list here as the list would be longer than the book itself. But I want you to know each of you has a special place in my heart.

Ted Foreman is a well-known "hockey guy" in Winnipeg and a lifelong friend. Ted took on the role of Bruce Oake fundraiser. He brokered a number of significant donations in addition to handing me a large personal cheque every time I met him for lunch.

Feeding fifty men three times a day is costly, and it works at Bruce Oake because of Pratt's Wholesale, owned and operated by Jeff, Leonard, and Jason Baranyk. The Baranyks provide our food at cost in addition to an ongoing financial commitment.

Transportation is important in recovery. Bruce Oake needs a way to get the men to and from meetings, work, and appointments. It took but one text to Mark and Steve Chipman for the Birchwood Auto Group to donate a fifteen-passenger van. Scott Campbell, the dealer principal at Midtown Ford, and owner Pat Priestner were just as generous, quick to give us a brand-new transit van in addition to a couple of large donations.

I know nothing about construction, but I do know we would have been lost without Joe Bova and Susan Russell. Joe is a longstanding veteran in the business, and we were fortunate to have him sign on as our project manager. Susan is a landscape architect who represented us at public information sessions and helped get us through the permit process, which can test anyone's patience.

I'm thankful for the work of Lesley Klink. Lesley, in the face of the early neighbourhood backlash, started, on her own initiative, the Friends of Bruce Oake Facebook page. She continues to administer it as well as sitting on our community committee.

Grief can get the better of a person, certainly if you lose your son and your wife. Mine hasn't, although I have my moments. Lots of things can trigger tears including many parts of this book. So, I can't say I've risen above my grief—only that I carry on. And that is possible because of the love and support of friends and colleagues like the ones at CBC Sports, *Hockey Night in Canada*, and Rogers Sportsnet. I won't list people here for fear of leaving someone out. I just want you to know that your support has played a huge role in saving lives at Bruce Oake and the ones that will be saved at the Anne Oake Family Recovery Centre.

And finally, I thank every person who has bought this book (and hopefully read it) as every penny of profit from it goes to the Bruce and Anne Oake Foundation. That means you're supporting men and women in their pursuit of recovery and the sober, healthy lives that go with it.

About the Authors

SCOTT OAKE is a Gemini Award–winning sportscaster for CBC Sports, Sportsnet, and *Hockey Night in Canada*. Raised in Sydney, Nova Scotia, he began his broadcasting career at Memorial University's campus radio station before going on to work with CBC for five decades. Oake has covered Canada's biggest sports moments, including the Olympics, Commonwealth Games, CFL football, in addition his longstanding role as part of *Hockey Night in Canada*. He is included on the Media Roll of Honour of the Manitoba Sportswriters and Sportscasters Association and has been appointed a Member of both the Order of Manitoba and the Order of Canada.

MICHAEL HINGSTON is the author of three books, and the coauthor of Harnarayan Singh's memoir, the national bestseller *One Game at a Time*. He is also the owner of Porch Light Books in Edmonton, Alberta.